THE THIRTEENITIES

LEADING TWEENS TO LIVES OF
GREATNESS AND GOODNESS

MARTTI PAJUNEN

The Thirteenities – Leading Tweens to Lives of Greatness and
Goodness
By Martti Pajunen

Copyright © 2017 by Martti Pajunen

All rights reserved. No part of this publication may be reproduced,
distributed, or transmitted in any form or by any means, including
photocopying, recording, or other electronic or mechanical meth-
ods, or by any information storage and retrieval system, without
the prior written permission of the publisher and author, except in
the case of brief quotations embodied in critical reviews and certain
other non-commercial uses permitted by copyright law.

ISBN: 978-1-944177-67-6 (P)
ISBN: 978-1-944177-68-3 (P)

Crescendo Publishing, LLC
300 Carlsbad Village Drive
Ste. 108A, #443
Carlsbad, California 92008-2999
1-877-757-8814

www.CrescendoPublishing.com
GetPublished@CrescendoPublishing.com

Printed in the United States of America
Cover design by Melody Hunter

10 9 8 7 6 5 4 3 2 1

The Thirteenities
[thur-TEEN-i-tees]

Leading tweens to lives of greatness and goodness.

A Message from the Author

*"There is no single effort more radical in its potential
for saving the world than a transformation
of the way we raise our children."*
– Marianne Williamson

My name is Martti Pajunen. Thank you for checking out *The Thirteenities*. Like the title of this book, parenting tweens - children from age nine to twelve - can be both confusing and fascinating. I believe that parents of tweens are provided an extraordinary opportunity in their role, to literally change the world.

For over twenty-five years I worked with tweens, adolescents, and their parents. During that time, I discovered firsthand that every parent wanted the same things for their children. They wanted their children to succeed and reach their full potential, but they also really wanted them to be decent citizens by living out time honored virtuous values. They may have stated those desires in different ways, but in the end, every parent I met just hoped their children would ultimately become adults who lived lives characterized by greatness and goodness.

I also discovered that many parents did not feel prepared or equipped for the task of parenting, especially when their children became teenagers. In fact, many of them started to prepare once their children were already adolescents. They were learning, but learning too late.

I wrote *The Thirteenities* to help parents of preadolescent children (aka tweens) prepare themselves and their children for the adolescent or teenage years.

Parents, my message to you is simply this: You can lead your children to lives of greatness and goodness by igniting and infusing in them virtuous values, not by attempting to modify their behavior through reward and punishment. In fact, through my research and personal experience, I discovered 13 transformational and interconnected values that a tween could begin to embrace that would set them on the path to success into their adolescent years and ultimately adulthood. I believe parents and children are gifts to each other. In the same way, a mature, responsible adult is truly a gift to the world.

I personally invite every parent to investigate *The Thirteenities*. The book and supplementary teaching is not quick fix or 3 step program to change the way your child behaves. In fact, it is much greater. It is a transformational approach to parenting that begins with changing our mindset as parents, not just trying to change our children.

The book is supported with an available online video training series for parents and with other resources designed to assist you through the preadolescent and teenage years. These can all be found on my website www.thethirteenities.com.

As a special way to say thank you for purchasing my book, I am pleased to give you a free gift - a Coming of Age Ceremony planning guide (PDF). This guide will help you plan and run a personalized coming of age ceremony for your son or daughter's 13th birthday.

To accept this gift, click on http://www.thethirteenities.com/bookgift.

My hope for you is that you will continue to find incredible joy in your children. I wish you extraordinary success as parents.

Table of Contents

CHAPTER 1: *INTRODUCTION*..*5*

CHAPTER 2: *WHAT ARE THE THIRTEENITIES?*...................*13*

CHAPTER 3: *THE PRESEASON*....................................... *27*

CHAPTER 4: *MATURITY*..*35*

CHAPTER 5: *RESPONSIBILITY*...................................... *45*

CHAPTER 6: *COMMUNITY*... *55*

CHAPTER 7: *GENEROSITY*... *65*

CHAPTER 8: *HUMILITY* *75*

CHAPTER 9: *INTEGRITY*..*83*

CHAPTER 10: *PURITY*..*89*

CHAPTER 11: *TENACITY* *95*

CHAPTER 12: *FLEXIBILITY* *103*

CHAPTER 13: *AUTHENTICITY* *111*

CHAPTER 14: *SPIRITUALITY*..119*

CHAPTER 15: *CURIOSITY* *127*

CHAPTER 16: *CREATIVITY* 135*

CHAPTER 17: *THE COMING OF AGE CEREMONY* *141*

CHAPTER 18: *FINALLY*...*147*

Dedication

I dedicate this book to my children—Mariah, Brianne, and Maxfield. For some reason, we ended up together as a family. I celebrate each of you in your uniqueness and beauty.

Although imperfect, I was always perfectly delighted to be your father.

Foreword

In most sports, there are three seasons: the preseason, the regular season, and the playoffs. The preseason is the time when coaches and players prepare for the regular season. The coaching staff communicates their vision and goals for the team for that season and confirms the values the team will embrace. They prepare for specific situations they will face throughout the season and practice the fundamentals of their sport. They work hard to prepare physically, mentally, and emotionally. They follow a specific training manual; and they have fun together. Each player is celebrated for the unique talents they bring to the team.

The Thirteenities is like a preseason training manual for parents whose children have not yet entered the teenage years. If you have, or soon will have, a tween, this book is for you. It will help you prepare for your child becoming a teenager and ultimately an independent, mature adult. The adolescent years are both fun and frightening for parents; and for their children. I believe it is an amazing season of life. A season of change and overcoming challenges. A season of growth and development. A season of struggle, success, and satisfaction. A true coming-of-age that everyone experiences. On behalf of your children, I want to thank you for taking the time and making the effort to prepare yourself and them for their teenage season.

CHAPTER 1

INTRODUCTION

*"We write in response to what we read and learn;
and in the end we write out of our deepest selves."*

– Andrea Barrett

Beginning

When I was a teenager, I was invited to become a volunteer youth worker for a group of eleven- and twelve-year-olds. I said "yes," and it changed my life forever. The leadership team of this group consisted of myself and two married couples. As I recall, one couple was in their thirties and the other in their fifties, although when you are a teenager, you consider anyone older than twenty to be pretty much ancient. The kids in the group were an eclectic collection to be sure. There were the twelve-year-old girls who were into cosmetics and the latest fashion, and there were the eleven-year-old boys who lived for biking and road hockey. Some were loud and outgoing, others shy and self-conscious, but they all seemed to like to have fun. We met every Wednesday evening in a small room in the basement of an older church building in uptown Waterloo, Ontario.

It was my job to lead some activities and games for the kids before the other leaders led a time of music, sharing, and teaching. Some nights I was like a cheerleader, motivating the kids to get involved in games they really didn't want to play. Other nights I was more of a referee, breaking up battles between them. More often than not, I was really just a babysitter. I made sure they didn't clog the toilets with toilet paper rolls or start teasing each other excessively for their choice of clothing. I remember those Wednesday evenings as a mixture of both joy and frustration, laughter and words of warning, the silly and the serious.

Little did I know that those few hours each week were a window into the unique world of the preadolescent. The time I spent planning and running activities with those kids became the seeds, water, and soil that grew into a career for the next twenty-five years of my life. In the decades that followed, I continued to fulfil my passion to work with children and adolescents in multiple capacities. I was a youth worker, volunteer high school counselor, mentor, event planner, out-trip leader, college professor, and keynote speaker to youth, parents, and youth leaders across North America. It has been an honor to have interacted with hundreds of youth workers and parents, and thousands of adolescent and preadolescent young people. I also experienced firsthand what it means to be the parent of a tween as I trekked with my own three children through their preadolescent and adolescent years. As a fellow traveler who has walked a few steps ahead, I am honored to share what I know and what I think I know about leading children in this weird, wacky, and wonderful age group.

Book

I wrote *The Thirteenities* simply to share some wisdom I have learned over the years in working with preadolescent children. Like many authors and teachers, some of my personal learning has come from reading, attending seminars, and observing life, but much of it has come through the challenges and mistakes I have made. It reminds me of the words from the highly successful NCAA and NBA basketball coach Rick Pitino, who said, "Failure is good. It's fertilizer. Everything I've learned about coaching, I have learned from making mistakes." If it's true that you learn from the mistakes you have made, I am the smartest person I know. There has been much fertilizer, and sometimes the smell still lingers. I have also learned from numerous women and men who possessed significant depth of insight into leading preadolescent children.

This book is meant to focus attention on what it means for parents to lead their tweenagers. One of the realities of this age group is that they are natural followers. They follow trends. They follow celebrities and peers. They are open to influence from those with leadership titles and positions, as well as those who lead without a title. Some are savvy, but most are easily influenced and often manipulated.

You are reading this book because you are a parent of one or more tweenagers (or more simply, "tweens"). Parents play many roles in the lives of their children. They must provide healthy and nutritional meals, comfort them when they are anxious, play with them, and protect them. But in my opinion, the most important role they play is leader. As such, they need to step up to that role in order to be the best they can be for their children. My hope is that this book and all the additional supporting resources will inspire you as a parent to become the leader you need you to be. Honestly, I wish someone else had written this book for me before I became the parent of a tween. It would have helped me to clarify my role as a parent and provided some much-needed direction and inspiration.

Back burner

For many people, their bucket list simply remains as words on a piece of paper, or more likely, a list that has not even been written down. This book has been a longtime dream of mine, but sadly, it remained a dream left on the back burner of my mind until September 24, 2014. For several years preceding that day, I had struggled with poor physical, emotional, and mental health.

An overwhelming and exhausting travel and work schedule consumed the summer of 2014. I was driving over 1,000 kilometers each week. Following one strenuous road trip, I noticed that my left leg had begun to swell up. For several days it continued to cause me some discomfort, but I kept putting off going to the doctor. Finally I phoned my oldest daughter, who just happens to be an ER nurse. I told her about my leg, and she insisted I go to the hospital immediately. Thankfully, I did.

After several hours of tests, an ultrasound, and bloodwork, the doctor met with me in a small treatment room. The conversation that followed is etched into my mind. He said, "Martti, you have a blood clot in your leg, and it is quite serious. Now, you have two choices. You can go home now, make no significant changes in your life, and you will die. And you may die fairly soon. Or, you can choose to live. We can get you on blood thinners right away, we can help you with your diet and exercise, and you will probably live to be an old man. So, what do you want to do? Do you want to live?"

In the quietness of that small, sterile room, I placed my head in my hands and sat in silence. I couldn't answer that question. I was at such a dark place in my life that I wasn't even sure I wanted to live. As I sat in that moment of stillness, many images passed through my mind, from my family and friends, to my success in my life as well as unfulfilled dreams. The images came and went. Then the slideshow suddenly stopped. In a moment of inexplicable peace, my mind paused, and I saw an image of the beautiful face of my granddaughter, Charleigh. She was just nine months old at that time. She was my first grandchild, and I was her poppa. I don't know why, but the image of her face froze on the screen of my mind. I will never forget it because that became a defining moment for me.

We all understand that there are no guarantees in life. None of us know for certain what will happen tomorrow. Our health and even our relationships can be very fragile. The steps of our journey can seem so uncertain. The struggles and challenges, so overwhelming. But at that moment, I made a decision that transformed my life. I decided to live. I chose life—for myself, and for her. I chose what I feel is the ultimate human accountability; I accepted full responsibility for my own life. Charleigh was just nine months old, but on that day, without even knowing it, she saved my life.

So, I looked up at the doctor and said, "I want to live."

Everyone remembers those inspirational, life-changing moments from the movies: the Mel Gibson "freedom" speech in *Braveheart* or the Al Pacino "inch by inch" speech from *Any Given Sunday*. I love those for sure. But the quiet and redemptive moments of transformation also inspire me, like Joaquin Phoenix and Reese Witherspoon's conversation in *Walk the Line* or Mark Wahlberg's "I'm not actually a gambler" revelation in *The Gambler*.

I believe that was my moment. When I spoke the words out loud, "I want to live," that was my emancipation. It was my speech to myself—an attentive audience of one. Four simple words. *I want to live.*

The doctor replied, "Good. Now we can help you."

That began an extraordinary rebirth in my life. With God's help and the support of my family and friends, I began a journey back to health and wholeness. I lost over fifty pounds, got an awesome tattoo, was taken off all medication, and wrote this book.

Some may think it's insensitive for a physician to ask such a question, "Do you want to live?" It sounds so inappropriate, so condescending and wrong. I see it differently. It was an invitation for me to take responsibility for myself. I truly believe everyone's life is a gift, including my own. A gift to be thankful for and celebrated, but also to be lived, enjoyed, and used to the fullest. So, this is a question I have asked myself every morning since that pivotal date. "Do I want to live?" And each day the answer has always been YES!

Do I want to live? Yes.

Do I want to really live? Yes.

Do I want to live the life for which I was created? Yes.

Do I want to bring life, hope, and joy into the lives of others? Yes.

Do I want to live even when life itself is disappointing and difficult? Yes.

Do I want to live today? Yes!

Do I want to live? Yeah!

Do I really, really want to live? Hell, yeah!

So, because I chose to live, I was able to write this book.

Insights

- My passion to influence young people and families actually began when I was just a teenager myself.

- You can receive direction and inspiration about parenting from my library of wisdom and learning from the mistakes I have made over the years.

- Because I accepted responsibility for myself and received a second chance in my own life, I am delighted to be able to share this book with you.

CHAPTER 2

WHAT ARE THE THIRTEENITIES?

"I have a dream ... that someday my children will be judged not by the color of their skin but rather by the content of their character."

– Dr. Martin Luther King Jr.

"There is no school equal to a decent home and no teacher equal to a virtuous parent."

– Mohandas Karamchand Gandhi

Words

The legendary actor and comedian Robin Williams once said, "No matter what people tell you, words and ideas can change the world." You have probably never heard the word "Thirteenities" before. That's because I made it up. I created it because there was no other word that quite explained what I observed to be true. This is my definition.

The Thirteenities are a collection of virtuous values that parents can ignite and infuse in the lives of tweens leading them toward lives of greatness and goodness.

The definition breaks down into several key thoughts.

Collection

Simply put, the Thirteenities are just thirteen words. There were others that could have made this list; however these, in my opinion, are the most important ones. As you read this book, you will discover that these words are not just words. They are life-changing ideas and values. You have probably used each of these words in your everyday conversation. You know what they mean. But I have discovered the Thirteenities are a library of words that belong together and support each other. They do stand alone, just like every finger on your hand is independent from the other. But they also cooperate organically, and that's where the real strength is found. Amazingly, when all your fingers work together, they are much stronger than just one working alone. The Thirteenities are thirteen powerful words that can work together to change the life of your tween ... forever.

Virtuous Values

The Thirteenities are virtuous values.

Values are the ideas, beliefs, or moral principles that are deemed most important to an individual or a group. Values are often specific to a people group, but even commonly shared values are sometimes expressed differently in different cultures. The core values we embrace always influence the decisions we make and the activities in which we take part. Our true values truly influence how we live and are often aligned with specific attachments. Possessions and money.

Prayer and worship. Leadership and power. Honesty and respect. Education and achievement.

We often incorrectly assume that just because someone has values, the values that they hold close are morally good or excellent. Not true. Some values are obviously unjust or lack essential goodness, such as the value of using physical strength to intimidate or bully others. That may be a value, but it is certainly not virtuous.

Virtues, on the other hand, are character qualities commonly accepted as being good or morally excellent, such as patience, justice, courage, and love. The original Latin word **_virtus_** meant "valor" or "moral perfection." Virtues certainly carry spiritual or religious overtones; however, they are generally accepted by most people as just being beneficial in the social development of all humans. The opposite of virtue is vice, a word that describes behaviors that are wicked or criminal. Vices also include any activity that is considered a bad habit.

I have fused these two words—"virtues" and "values"—together to communicate that the Thirteenities are both values that are good and virtues that should be important. Hence, virtuous values.

Parents

The Thirteenities is written for parents of children ages nine to twelve, or "tweens". Because tweens normally depend on someone else to meet their financial, emotional, and physical needs, they require adults to provide for them.

The primary providers for tweens are their biological parents, but they can also include stepparents, legal guardians, foster parents, or godparents. Anyone who is the 24/7 provider and who is ultimately responsible for meeting the basic needs of a child acts as a parent.

In addition to parents, many other significant adults act as secondary and supportive providers. I like to call these people "gatekeepers." Gatekeepers are adults who are responsible for supporting parents by providing physical care, education, emotional support, oversight, and leadership to their preadolescent child. Gatekeepers include teachers, youth workers, club leaders, coaches, instructors, health care professionals, clergy and religious leaders, civic leaders, extended family members, neighbors, and other significant adults. A gatekeeper is someone who oversees and guards what information, images, and impressions are allowed to enter the heart and mind of a tween. Parents are obviously active in providing those things but do often outsource that responsibility to others.

Parents and gatekeepers help to shape the character of a tween. They introduce and affirm a moral framework and help to teach and affirm values. The role that parents and gatekeepers play in the lives of tweenagers is critical because once a tween is influenced in a certain direction, they can stay on that course for the rest of their lives. Tweens are constantly forming habits that they will carry with them through the adolescent years into adulthood.

I worked at a children's camp in Huntsville, Ontario, for two summers during my college years. One of my roles there was to lead the camp sailing program. Each of the tiny sailboats was designed for just one child, although many times the kids wanted to double up just to be with their friends. The sailboats had two significant parts that actually went below the surface of the water—the keel and the rudder. The keel, or centerboard, is the part that protrudes down from the middle of the hull and is designed to counteract sideways movement. The rudder is the appendage at the stern, or the back of the sailboat, that is designed to steer the boat. The keel and rudder work together to keep the boat upright and moving in the desired direction. In fact, the campers learned quickly how to sail regardless of the direction of the wind. Unfortunately, the centerboards were removable, so sometimes the campers pulled them out and used them like oars to splash their friends. (Go figure—tweens found a way to have fun.) Water wars on Mary Lake would arise. The kids had an absolute blast having fun together, but because the keels had been removed, the boats would drift into the reeds near the shore and they would get trapped. Thankfully, "Boomer" (my camp nickname) came to the rescue, and I helped them get back to safety.

I believe that parents and gatekeepers are the keels and rudders in the lives of tweens. Their role is to provide stability and direction for them, regardless of the winds, waves, and changing currents of the culture. Their investment is significant in helping children develop their character and avoid drifting into danger during these critical years.

Ignite and infuse

The Thirteenities are life-changing. It is a worthy objective for a parent to both live them out and to download them into the life of their tween. The process of passing on these values is both challenging and time-consuming. Parenting is often a thankless career choice.

I have observed that there are two primary words that describe how these values are passed on—"ignite" and "infuse."

When a firecracker fuse is ignited, an explosion follows. The effect is immediate and memorable. The memories are often pleasant, but sometimes things go sideways and the result is pain...and a story to tell. Sometimes an event occurs in the life of a preadolescent that causes immediate and permanent life transformation. These events could be intentional or accidental, but they are explosive.

One such event was the sudden and unexpected death of a classmate of mine when I was in grade eight. The boy's name was Dan. We were in a phys ed class doing a warm-up run before we got into our main activities. I had already returned inside to the gym when someone ran in and said that Dan had collapsed. I do not recall everything that followed; it was all a blur. All I know is that, sadly, my classmate Dan died that day.

Up to that point in my life, I personally knew only one other individual in the entire world who had died, my great-aunt Edna. She died when I was just eleven years old. She was seventy-five. So I knew that people died, but I did not really comprehend that a child could. I thought it was just old people. Those two events occurred within two years of each other, but they helped to ignite the value of maturity within me. My gatekeepers (teachers, school counselors, clergy, and youth workers) and my parents helped me to better understand the realities and mysteries of death. As a result, I become more mature. Maturity traffics in reality and sometimes that reality is harsh. Those two deaths, and the insight I gained from my parents and gatekeepers, informed me that life is not just fun and games. And it was not forever. Death has a way of helping us all to better appreciate life. Those events and the follow-up conversations helped ignite that virtuous value within me.

More commonly, however, these values are infused into the lives of tweens. Infuse means to pour in, to cause to be permeated, or to introduce one thing into another so as to change it forever. Tea leaves are infused in hot water to change the composition of the beverage, a music teacher can infuse confidence into their students, or a grandmother can infuse unconditional love (and sugary treats) into her grandchildren. Having observed parents and tweens for almost three decades, I am convinced that the best way for values to be transferred to tweens is for parents to model them consistently and congruently. Adults who live so that their beliefs, their words, and their actions are all in alignment influence children the most. Igniting happens immediately and is often unplanned. Infusing is the long-term modeling of values by a parent. It is a slow, often uneventful instilling of values from a parent to a child that will change the life of that child forever. The Thirteenities are ignited and infused into the lives of tweens.

Tweens

What is a tween? I have been using the term already, so a definition now will certainly be helpful. The term "tween" was really first coined by J.R.R. Tolkien in his 1954 novel *The Fellowship of the Ring*. In his book, Tolkien describes a Hobbit between the ages of twenty and thirty-three as a tween because, as we all know, thirty-three is the time of a Hobbit's coming-of-age. That is not the definition I will be using for this book.

Although there is not full agreement on the exact definition, the general consensus is that a tween is a person who is living between childhood and adolescence, literally in be-"tween" being a child and a teenager, a child who is on the edge of puberty. I would suggest it describes the three to four years before puberty takes place. Tweens can be defined as being between the ages of nine and twelve years old, or in grades four to seven in school in North America. Other words used to describe this group are "tweenagers," "preadolescents," "early adolescents," "students," "children," and "monsters." A lot of good information is available on the lowering age puberty in North America. I encourage parents and gatekeepers to be aware of this fascinating trend.

The tween years, much like the teen years, include a broad range of members. Tweens will vary significantly in body size, emotional maturity, intelligence, and general appearance. Personally, I like the term. It carries a certain ambiguity and awkwardness that could be used to describe anyone that is in between something like a job or romantic relationship. A fun exercise for parents of tweens is to find some photos or even a yearbook from when they were in that age group. After the initial shock wave of embarrassment recedes from seeing those photos, you will be reminded of what it was like to be a tween.

Leading them

Teachers teach, coaches coach, singers sing, and parents parent. The first three are easily understandable; the fourth is a bit trickier. What does it mean to parent? What does "parent" in the verb form actually mean?

Wikipedia says, "Parenting or child rearing is the process of promoting and supporting the physical, emotional, social, financial, and intellectual development of a child from infancy to adulthood. Parenting refers to the aspects of raising a child aside from the biological relationship."

A long list of general things parents do for their children includes the following: provide, teach, correct, affirm, set limits, encourage, celebrate, prepare, and love. When it comes to values, I remind parents that their primary responsibility is to lead their tweens. Parenting is leadership. I have read dozens of books on organizational and personal leadership, and there is no end to the number of definitions. That said, here are two definitions I like:

"Leadership is the capacity to translate vision into reality." (Warren Bennis)

"Leadership is influence—nothing more, nothing less." (John Maxwell)

I believe the primary role that parents should play in the lives of their tweens is that of leader. Good leaders set the agenda, move their followers toward a clear, compelling vision of a preferred future, and inspire their followers to join them on that quest. Parents can and should do the same with their children. You may say, "I am not a natural leader. I am more of a follower." In the general activities of life, that may be an acceptable opt-out. However, when it comes to parenting, my three decades of experience screams: "Be one anyway!" Good parenting always means good leadership within the family context. An eight-year-old should not tell a parent what their bedtime is. A nine-year-old should not be given unlimited freedom to eat whatever and whenever they want. A ten-year-old should not be responsible for paying the rent or mortgage. Those responsibilities belong to the leaders in the family—the parents. One of the greatest lessons parents need to learn is that they are the leaders. Parents lead their tweens.

Greatness and goodness

I have spoken with some parents who have very specific dreams and goals for their children: To succeed at a particular sport. To pursue a specific career. To apply to the college or university they attended. To become wealthier or more successful than they are. One parent of a teenage boy once told me that his goal for his son was that he would just avoid jail and not get his girlfriend pregnant. Unfortunately, his son achieved neither of those goals.

Most parents have a more common vision for their kids. They want them to be happy, to reach their potential, to find love, to enjoy the friendships of others, to find fulfillment, and "just to turn out OK." I have yet to meet the parent of a ten-year-old who would say, "My dream is that my daughter would fail at school, not be able to hold a job, regularly make poor decisions, and live a life filled with regrets."

Over the years, I have discovered that parents really just want two things for their children. They may say it in different ways, but the sentiment is always the same. They want their children to be great and to be good.

I love motorcycles. I have enjoyed riding through the beautiful backroads of Ontario in the autumn as well as beside the Atlantic Ocean in Florida. I enjoy riding alone or with others. I love the brotherhood and sisterhood of fellow bikers. I love that some bikers look like Santa Claus or Colonel Sanders. But most of all, I love the sound of motorcycles. I love the awesome, throaty rumble produced by the V-twin motorcycle engine. I know it annoys some, but I love it. It is the sound of happiness, love, and all things good.

The V-twin engine used by several motorcycle companies is made with two twin cylinders that are manufactured in the shape of a V—therefore, the name "V-twin." Both sides of this engine make it work the way it is supposed to work; both cylinders are necessary.

The same could be said of greatness and goodness. They work in harmony. They are powerful because they work together.

Parents want their children to be great, to succeed in life. They want them to become independent and able to support themselves. They want them to reach their potential. They want them to live with a sense of fulfillment in that their lives are full of the satisfaction that comes with achievement and accomplishment. They want them to discover and use their gifts, interests, and aptitudes to become the best version of themselves in their relationships, work, recreation, artistic expressions, and all their life ambitions. Parents want their children to be great. I did. I believe we all do.

But we also want our children to be good. In their pursuit of success, parents want their kids to embrace virtues like honesty, compassion, fairness, respect, and courage. They want them to be successful, but not at any cost. They don't want them to win the basketball game by breaking the rules. They don't want them to pass a test by cheating. They understand there is a greatness in goodness itself. So greatness and goodness combine to become the vision most parents have for their children.

The vision is clear: greatness and goodness.

But there's a problem.

What does it mean to be both great and good? What values support this vision parents have for their children? What specific strategies can be employed to achieve greatness and goodness in our children?

This is where the Thirteenities come in. They sharpen the focus for parents. They help them identify areas where their child can move toward the vision of greatness and goodness. They help parents take the next step in leading their children toward this vision. This step is often missing or unclear for most parents. The Thirteenities assist in bridging the gap between the vision parents have for their children and the strategy of day-to-day parenting. From my experience, the Thirteenities help define what it means to be great and good without making the practice of parenting too rigid. They leave much room for parents to determine what it will look like in their family, but they also bring clarity to the process of leading children.

For example, parents who want their children to become great and good often embrace the virtuous value of responsibility (one of the Thirteenities). But how a child lives out that value will differ from family to family. Some parents might say it means making your bed every morning or brushing your teeth every night. Others might say it means feeding the goldfish and having all your homework completed by eight o'clock each night. These specifics are what I call the vitality in parenting. Parenting has always been life-on-life influence. It should not be imposing robotic rules through punishment and reward.

It is more of a dance that involves flow, rhythm, movement, and occasionally stepping on toes. It is like a garden where growth takes place in the best environment. It is the messy, unpredictable, and ever-changing experience of parents giving their lives to lead their children. It is truly vitality.

Here's the equation: the vision of seeing children move toward goodness and greatness is enhanced by understanding how to ignite and infuse these virtuous values (the Thirteenities) into the lives of tweens, which leads to vitality in parenting.

Good parenting includes vision, values, and vitality.

Take a moment to read that again because many parents miss it. In parenting, the vision is enhanced by the values, which leads to the vitality.

It is as if the vision of greatness and goodness is written in permanent marker; the virtuous values are written in pen, but the vitality of parenting is written in pencil with a large eraser. That way the parenting strategies can be adjusted as needed. As I have explained this concept to parents, I have seen a renewed enthusiasm for their role as leaders in the lives of their tweens. That enthusiasm brings energy, passion, and vitality to parents—things we could all use more of ... agreed? Can you hear the V-twin begin to rumble?

This is an overview of what each of the Thirteenities means. These will be discussed in the coming chapters.

Maturity: I am becoming the best of what it means to be fully human.

Responsibility: I will take care of myself, my stuff, and my assignments.

Community: I will be a connected and contributing member of my tribe.

Generosity: I will use what I have to help others in need.

Humility: I will cultivate an attitude of thankfulness.

Integrity: I will say and do what is right and honorable.

Purity: I will fill my mind with what is true and wholesome.

Tenacity: I will not give up or give in.

Flexibility: I will adapt to change.

Authenticity: I will be the best version of my true self.

Spirituality: I will seek to discover the meaning of life.

Curiosity: I will continue to learn.

Creativity: I will express myself.

Insights

- *The Thirteenities* are a collection of virtuous values that parents can ignite and infuse in the lives of tweens leading them toward lives of greatness and goodness. *The Thirteenities* is both the title of the book and the name of the actual thirteen virtuous values. Tweens are children between the ages of 9 – 12 years old.

- Parents are the main influence in the lives of their tweens but do often outsource that responsibility to others, who I call "gatekeepers". These are people who oversee and guard what information, images, and impressions are allowed to enter the heart and mind of your tween.

- The main role of parents is to lead their children. The journey is toward both greatness and goodness.

CHAPTER 3

THE PRESEASON

"Spectacular achievement is always preceded by unspectacular preparation."

– Robert H. Schuller

"It is easier to build strong children than to repair broken men."

– Fredrick Douglass.

Development

I mentioned in the beginning of the book that in most sports, there are three seasons: the preseason, the regular season, and the playoffs. The preseason is the time when coaches and players prepare for the regular season. It is wise for parents to prepare specifically for the teenage years, and this book will help. The second decade of life is arguably the most changing and challenging, so parents need to be ready when their child reaches that stage. For us humans, there are several clearly defined stages of development. Authors such as Eric Erikson and Thomas Armstrong have identified these different stages of development through which every person must pass. Here is a brief overview of their models.

Eric Erikson
Infancy (birth to eighteen months)
Early childhood (eighteen months to three years)
Play age (three to five years)
School age (five to twelve years)
Adolescence (twelve to eighteen years)
Young adult (eighteen to forty years)
Adulthood (forty to sixty-five years)
Maturity (over sixty-five years)

Thomas Armstrong
Pre-birth
Birth
Infancy (zero to three years)
Early childhood (three to six years)
Middle childhood (six to eight years)
Late childhood (nine to eleven years)
Adolescence (twelve to twenty years)
Early adulthood (twenty to thirty-five years)
Midlife (thirty-five to fifty years)
Mature adulthood (fifty to eighty years)
Late adulthood (over eighty years)
Death and dying

Parents need to remember that each stage of development is indeed a stage. Childhood, the tween years, and the adolescent years all have a start and finish. Now, the beginning and end are always gradual, not abrupt. But there is definitely an end ... I promise you. When it comes to the tween years, I defer to the wisdom of the ancients who wrote, "This, too, will pass."

Parents should invest time and energy to prepare for each stage of their child's life leading up to adulthood. The success of the best-selling book *What to Expect When You're Expecting* demonstrates that expecting parents desire to be ready when their baby arrives on the scene. That same desire ought to be obvious in preparation for each development stage.

For parents of tweens, there is a simple explanation of what to expect when your child enters their teenage years. The key word here is "change." Significant, unstoppable, life-altering change. In fact, the changes that take place during the adolescent years are probably trumped only by the changes that take place in the human body during the forty prenatal weeks.

The teenage years see change primarily in the following four areas: body, mind, emotions, and relationships.

Body

The most obvious visible change a teenager experiences is in their body. Puberty, which signals the start of these changes, occurs between the ages of ten and thirteen (although there has been a drop in those ages in the past few decades). As puberty begins, hormones are released and the body changes, starting with the male and female sex organs. These begin to develop and eventually become capable of reproduction. Other changes naturally follow. For girls these include breast development, widening of the hips, the appearance of pubic and underarm hair, and the production of eggs from the ovaries as menstruation starts. For boys, the changes include the deepening of the voice, hair growth on the face and body, muscle increase, the development of the genitals, and production of sperm.

These changes are universal; every child on the planet will experience them. These changes will start and will continue until full physical maturity is achieved. It's like your child is driving a car up a ramp and onto a one-way multilane superhighway. The traffic is heavy and moving very fast. The road has numerous twists and turns, bumps and potholes, tunnels and steep hills, and there are no exits until you reach the final destination. There may be a few moments of fascination, but it's mostly fear, anxiety, and shock. Plus, everyone is checking out all the other cars. Parents, as your child's body begins to change, it's like your tween is almost at the on-ramp to the teenage autobahn. You will both need to buckle up.

Mind

The human brain is not fully developed until about age twenty-four; however, significant development takes place in the adolescent years. The abilities to take in new information, process thoughts logically, and remember more data all increase dramatically in the early to middle adolescent years. Early teenagers begin to understand abstract concepts as opposed to just concrete thoughts. They also become more open to entertaining new ideas and opinions. The views they have held since childhood have been challenged and have changed. Santa Claus, the Tooth Fairy, and even the boogieman have all returned to their place as mythical storybook characters. That is not to say that fantasy becomes irrelevant for tweens or teens. On the contrary, it becomes even more prominent, as is verified by the popularity of fantasy series like *The Lord of the Rings*, *A Series of Unfortunate Events*, and *Harry Potter*. The image of the teenage mind is like that of a sponge, soaking up and storing a sea of data from multiple sources. Their capacity to learn is extraordinary. Plus, teenagers rarely forget that you said they could use the car on Saturday night ... a statement you made three weeks ago.

Emotions

"The Mighty Canadian Minebuster™ is one of 3 wooden roller coasters at Paramount Canada's Wonderland and one of the original 4 roller coasters that were at the Park when it opened in 1981. It is the longest single track wooden coaster in Canada

at 3559 feet (1,085M). A modified traditional "Out & Back" wooden coaster which features an upward spiraling helix, the ride was built by Curtis T. Summers and was modeled after a ride at Coney Island."

That is the best image for describing what the emotions of an early adolescent can be, from laughter to tears, empathy to indifference, love to distain. Teenage emotions can change rapidly and in intensity in the blink (or wink) of an eye. Their need for acceptance and security opens the door for emotional manipulation, and sometimes their decisions are made in haste. The good news is that as they move into later adolescence and young adulthood, the emotional roller-coaster track becomes more level.

Relationships

A couple key relational transitions occur during adolescence. One is witnessing the number of significant peer friendships decrease from the tween years to the teen years. It's not that teens lose their friendships; rather they become more selective when it comes to who their close friends will be. Tweens are more group focused, but that group gets smaller as they move into the middle adolescent years and is most often based on sports, music, or some other affinity. During that transition, students accept greater autonomy and begin to choose their friends.

The second major change is seeing peers replace parents as the more significant influence in the life of a teenager. Parents are still very important to both tweens and teens, but the further into adolescence they move, the more dominant peer potency becomes. It's like an old playground teeter-totter, with a child on one side and the parents on the other. The relational weight obviously slants toward the parents at this time. But as the teen's group of friends increases and they jump on the child's side of the teeter-totter, the relational weight shifts and the parents get left "up in the air."

Parents of tweens have asked me, "What will the teenage years be like?" I just tell them it's like a highway, a sponge, a roller coaster, and a teeter-totter. Then they walk away ... and sometimes quietly weep.

Insights

- The teenage years see change primarily in the following four areas: body, mind, emotions, and relationships.

- All tweens will eventually develop and grow to become teenagers and their lives will then be like a highway, a sponge, a roller coaster, and a teeter-totter. The adolescent stage of life is a temporary one, so don't give up even if life becomes challenging.

- The influence of parents in the life of their tweens will gradually give way to the influence of the friends in the lives of their teens

CHAPTER 4

MATURITY

*"Maturity is achieved when a person postpones
immediate pleasures for long-term values."*
– Joshua L. Liebman

*"Parents can only give good advice or put them
on the right paths, but the final forming of a
person's character lies in their own hands."*
– Anne Frank

**Maturity: I am becoming the best of what it means to
be fully human.**

Best

The first and principal value parents should desire for their
tweens is maturity. All other values in this book flow from
this one. Unfortunately, maturity has a poor reputation. For
many tweens, maturity means boring, old, irrelevant—just
not fun. Some tweens have looked at adults who have acted
immaturely or inappropriately and have unfairly drawn the

conclusion that all adults are like that. They have seen the dark side of adulthood and said, "If that's what it means to be a grown-up, count me out. I'll hold onto my youth as long as I can."

Unfortunately, movies, sitcoms, and advertising support this negative stereotype of adulthood by portraying the parents or adults as idiots.

This is not what it means to be mature.

The word literally means "ripe, fully developed, or having reached maximum potential." It does mean grown-up, but I much prefer the idea of growing to reach your fullest potential. That communicates that maturity is a desirable value, which it really is. A leader in my area often uses the phrase "becoming the best version of yourself." I think that's what maturity can mean: Being independent and self-reliant. Having the ability to acquire resources and then knowing how to handle them. Having the freedom to make one's own decisions but also having the wisdom to know how to make the best decisions. Maturity means reaching the fullest potential in every area of life.

Now, that does not happen in the tween years. Moments in your tween's life will foreshadow that, but complete maturity only happens when we become adults. Whatever a child wants to do in their life, they will be able to do it to the best and fullest when they are adults. So as grown-ups, we should invite and welcome children into this world and teach them about what it means to be an adult. We should celebrate with them as they become the best of what it means to be human. We look forward to the day when they step out into the world as independent, self-sustaining, productive, mature adults— being the best they can be.

All the other Thirteenities flow from the value of maturity. It is most closely connected to responsibility, integrity, and authenticity, and as you will see, each of those have three connected values that flow from them as well. Although the connections are more like a web than a neatly designed flow chart, there seem to be streams that do flow together organically.

ABCD

Maturity reveals itself in four ways: attitudes, behavior, conversation, and decisions.

The attitude a tween demonstrates can reveal glimpses of maturity. Having an attitude of thankfulness, confidence, enthusiasm, compassion, helpfulness, friendliness, acceptance, teamwork, and even anger toward injustice all reveal a sense of maturity. John Maxwell says, "The greatest day in your life and mine is when we take total responsibility for our attitudes. That's the day we truly grow up." Although maturity is a process that is never fully completed, our attitude toward life discloses the degree of maturity we enjoy.

The behavior or actions of a preadolescent child often expose their level of maturity. When a tween opens a door for someone, completes a school assignment on time, or recycles their beverage bottle, they are behaving with age-appropriate maturity.

When I faced the reality of the death of my grade-eight classmate, I didn't know how to react because I had never been in that situation before. My response was simply that I didn't want to say or do the wrong thing. As I look back, I think that was actually an age-appropriate, mature response under the circumstances. It is interesting that over the years I have become more familiar with death and dying. As a funeral celebrant, I have conducted over 700 funerals, memorials, and celebration-of-life services. Sadly, some of those have been for tweens who have died. At the start of those unbelievably difficult services, I tell the story of my first experience with the death of my classmate in grade eight. I remind both the children and adults in attendance that at a time like this, we should never be ashamed, apologetic, or embarrassed of the tears we shed or the laughter we share. These behaviors are all part of what makes us human. Sometimes tweens just need permission from a trusted adult to remind them that their behavior is not bad or wrong; it's just age appropriate and natural. I reassure parents that their children's immature activities are part of the growing process and that they should celebrate the small changes in their kids' behavior.

The conversations and language a tween uses communicate (excuse the pun) their maturity. Someone once said our words are like bricks. We can use them in a productive way and build things, or we can use them in a destructive way and throw them to break things. Tweens love to chat and connect socially with each other. Parents can help their tweens understand the destructive nature of gossip, using hurtful words, blurting out profanity, lying, talking back, or yelling out putdowns with the goal of hurting others. Tweens can also learn the value of listening to others and allowing those who may be shy to join in a conversation as well. We have two ears and one mouth for a reason.

Finally, the decisions a tween makes reveal their stage of maturity. We all know that life is simply a series of choices and trade-offs. We cannot do everything we want to do. The decisions we make and when we make them always expose our priorities. If we choose to eat something spicy before going to bed, we expose our priority of enjoying food over getting a good night's sleep. Mature decisions are always rooted in delayed gratification over immediate pleasure. They also confirm a willingness to accept the natural consequences of the decision. When parents and tweens discuss a decision that needs to be made, often the choices are not between what is right and wrong, but between what is good and best. When a tween chooses right over wrong and what is best over what is just mediocre, they are deciding maturely.

Parents will observe the ABCDs of maturity in the lives of their tweens and see them growing in those areas: attitudes, behavior, conversation, and decisions. These will not always grow equally, but growth will take place and it will be noticeable.

Tug-of-war

Maturity, like all the Thirteenities, involves a tug-of-war.

For those who have never experienced tug-of-war, it is one of those rare, highly competitive games that seems to require little athletic ability whatsoever. In fact, the casual observer may believe it can be mastered by those who are terribly out of shape.

The object of tug-of-war is to join your teammates by grabbing one end of a heavy rope and pulling for all you are worth because there is another team on the other side doing the same thing. Hence, the tugging. The word "war" seems a bit extreme to describe the competitive nature of this activity, but as most tweens know, the more extreme the activity sounds, the better it probably is. Competitive tug-of-war has rules, guidelines, and referees. The recreational version is more of a free-for-all where, instead of using flags and a centerline to identify the winner, there is usually just a mud puddle. The losers are the ones who get tugged into a gooey mud mixture and become like those "before" photos in laundry detergent commercials. I much prefer the nonofficial category. What other sport can offer more fun than tug-of-war? You get to be with your friends, hang onto a rope, and try to pull other people face-first into the mud. This should be an Olympic event.

The maturity tug-of-war starts in the tween years and continues for at least a decade but probably longer. There will be days when your child lives to the best of their potential for their age, and then there will be other days when it seems they have slipped back into infancy. This is just the natural development process. There is no maturity pill they can take to make it happen immediately. It is helpful for parents to remember that the vision of greatness and goodness for your child will be best served as you ignite and infuse the value of maturity, and even then, children will resist it. In fact, there seems to be a common temptation for some older adolescents to resist maturity and independence.

Even when they have reached their twenties, some find it easier to simply stay at home, remaining dependent on the free food and accommodations that their parents have provided for many years already. This staying versus going is a tug-of-war. We need to understand, however, that it is maturity itself that pulls us toward adulthood and independence. Immaturity pulls back. Maturity reminds us that life's greatest lessons are learned in the difficulties and challenges of life, not in the comfort of the classroom or the bedroom or the basement of the family home. Maturity invites us to become the best version of ourselves, while immaturity tempts us to extend our adolescence well into our adulthood.

Comedian Alonzo Bowden once said, "Parents can encourage their children to go to college, go to university, go to the military, or go right into the workforce. The goal and key word, however, is always: GO!"

Fun

It is and should be fun to be a tween. It is also fun to be an adolescent and an adult, but it is a different kind of fun. Tween fun is mostly self-centered and often very crazy—sneaking out at night to play a prank on your friends, having marathon video-game sessions, eating tons of candy and junk food, and telling fart jokes. It is childishness, silliness, and goofiness. Those, by the way, are all amazing ways for children to enjoy life. Kids should be allowed to be kids. Let me say that again: kids should be allowed to be kids. Kid fun, enjoyed by kids, is normal.

There is a time, however, when fun becomes more mature. Fun, like love, carries a deeper level of satisfaction as we grow up. It becomes more childlike than childish. Fun can actually become mature. On a weekend retreat I ran at a conference center in Ontario, a group of teenagers and their adult leaders pulled off an amazing prank. The dining room at the conference center was set up at night in preparation for breakfast the next day. The plates, cutlery, and coffee cups were all in place on the round dining room tables. These clever pranksters snuck into the dining room, removed all the round tables, and reset all the place settings, salt and pepper shakers, and napkin dispensers on the floor exactly below where they would have been on the tables. Over 150 place settings were set on the floor, and it looked like the tables had simply vanished. It was spectacular! When the guests and kitchen staff came in early the next morning, they were shocked to see the prank; it was one of the highlights of the weekend.

The story didn't end there as the prankers revealed who they were and then worked to reset the room to its original pre-pranked state. The prank was epic, but the cleanup of the prank was epic maturity. The group understood that their fun should not cause others to have less fun, so they cleaned up. Kudos to that group.

Tween fun involves playing games; adult fun is providing an environment where tweens can play their games. Tween fun is going to a week of summer camp. Mature fun is leading a fundraiser so that tweens who could not afford to go to camp, now have that opportunity. Tween fun is laughing at others; mature fun is being able to laugh at yourself.

Ideas for igniting and infusing maturity into your tween

- Give your tween a brick to be used as a door stopper or bookend. Let them know that the brick is a reminder to use their words as bricks to build up, not to destroy.

- Ask your tween, "Of all the adults you know, who would you like most to be like and why?" Use that as a conversation to help you understand what your tween thinks about adulthood.

- Talk to your tweens about the experiences you have had with the deaths of your family members or friends. Share honestly with them your feelings and fears, your grief and comfort, and how you moved forward. For older tweens, you may want to actually visit a funeral home or meet with a funeral director to discuss the reality of death. This exercise must be done with great care and appropriateness, but I believe exposing children to the realities of life and death, in the safety of the thoughtfulness and wisdom of parents, is of great value.

- Write down several ways your child has demonstrated a greater level of maturity in the past year. Commit to verbally expressing affirmation and appreciation to your child for what you have observed.

Insights

- Maturity is the principal value parents should desire of their children. It means that I am becoming the best of what it means to be fully human.

- Maturity reveals itself in four ways: attitudes, behavior, conversation, and decisions.

- The maturity tug-of-war means that children will resist embracing personal maturity sometimes. This is just a natural part of the development process.

CHAPTER 5

RESPONSIBILITY

*"Success on any major scale requires
you to accept responsibility...
In the final analysis, the one quality that
all successful people have...
is the ability to take on responsibility."*

– Michael Korda

*"My belief is that personal freedom cannot grow
beyond personal responsibility. The more people
that learn to be fully accountable for their lives,
the more freedom each of us can enjoy and
the more fulfilling all of our lives will be."*

– Ross Parmenter

Responsibility: I will take care of myself, my stuff, and my assignments.

Me

Responsibility is like the firstborn child of maturity. This value informs us that our first priority is to take care of ourselves, our stuff, and our assignments. Tweens are at the stage of life when they can start taking on greater responsibility in those three areas. They can take more initiative in caring for their bodies and health through wise choices related to diet, exercise, sleep, and managing stress. They can learn how to care for their possessions without becoming materialistic or addicted to consumerism. And they can learn that in life there are often duties they are obligated to perform and that completing them with excellence is often the pathway to success.

Whenever we fly on a commercial airline, we listen (or don't) to the preflight instructions from the flight crew. One of the safety instructions is related to the "unlikely" event that the cabin should lose pressure. In that case the oxygen masks will drop from the ceiling, and we are to place them over our mouths, tighten the straps, and breathe normally. The next instruction goes something like this: "If you are travelling with small children, put **your** oxygen mask on first before you assist them with **theirs.**" Good advice. Your primary responsibility is yourself first, your children second. The point is simply this: if we don't take responsibility for ourselves, we will not be any good to anyone else.

Responsibility operates that way. It reminds us that as we take care of ourselves first, we are then invited to take care of other responsibilities and bigger tasks, including helping others.

A tween who takes care of their clothing or musical instrument may be ready to take care of a pet. The one who completes their schoolwork on time and arrives early for their soccer practice may be ready for a weekend away at their cousin's home. Demonstrating responsibility for themselves, their stuff, and their assignments will allow tweens to enjoy more privileges.

Parents can lead their tweens in understanding what responsibility is by informing them that responsibility and freedom go hand in hand. The more responsible a person becomes, the more freedom they can enjoy. This life principle is uniquely illustrated in the May 8, 2005, story of the Statue of Responsibility by Caleb Warnock published in the Daily Herald of Provo, Utah. The story speaks of the creation of a 300-foot stainless steel monument on the west coast of the United States, called the Statue of Responsibility. This monument was established to bookend the Statue of Liberty on the east coast. The project was inspired by Viktor Frankl in his best-selling book, *Man's Search for Meaning*, where he wrote, "Freedom is not the last word. Freedom is only part of the story and half of the truth." The statues were to complement each other and remind us that freedom must always walk hand in hand with responsibility.

Freedom can be achieved through living responsibly. But as someone once said, "Most people do not really want freedom, because freedom involves responsibility, and most people are frightened of responsibility." Parents can help lessen those fears as they help their tweens understand responsibility. We tend to fear less the things we understand.

Backpacks

Parents of school-age children are familiar with the backpack. These carry-all bags that are strapped to the spines of young students are often adorned with cartoon characters or action figures. Filled with school supplies, books, clothing, and lunches, they enable children to transport their gear both to and from school. I have purchased numerous backpacks for my own children over the years as they prepared to start a new school year. The trick is to make sure they not only like the look of the backpack, but that it is sized right for their bodies and the volume of supplies they will be carrying.

I think backpacks represent responsibility.

They remind us that each individual has a responsibility to carry her own supplies. On numerous occasions I have witnessed parents actually carry their child's backpack to school for them. Let me say that again: I have witnessed parents actually carry their child's backpack to school for them. They may think they are helping their children, but in fact they are hindering their development of personal responsibility. Let them carry their own backpack! Wow, I can almost hear my dad's voice when I type this.

"But it's heavy." If it's too heavy, get rid of some of the contents.

"But it's not fun for them." Great, as they walk to school, they are learning that all of life is not fun—bonus learning before the school bell rings.

"But other parents carry their children's backpack." Seriously? You are giving in to parental peer pressure? Grow up! Again, my father's voice echoes here.

Backpacks and their contents change over the years. As a schoolchild moves on from grade to grade, their backpacks change from being decorated with primary cartoon characters, to clothing brands and sports fashion. The contents change from crayons and crafts to calculus books and computers. Responsibilities change over time as well—from picking up toys to picking up a paycheck.

The skill of leadership parenting is understanding the level of responsibility your child has reached and relating to them appropriately. Parents must not overpack their tweens' lives with too much responsibility, but they must remind them there are loads they must carry on their own.

Expectations

Responsibility must always start with a clear understanding of expectations. Clarity is critical. I grew up playing minor hockey in Kitchener. Like all team sports, hockey demands that each player understands their role and takes their responsibility seriously. For instance, my coaches taught me that on a two-on-one rush, the defenseman must always take away the potential pass between the forwards so the goalie can focus on the player with the puck. If that expectation is fulfilled, the chances of the team scoring a goal is greatly reduced. However, if a goal is scored, the defenseman will not be held accountable because they fulfilled their role and did what they were supposed to do. Successful teams have players who are coached to be responsible for their roles, regardless of their skill level. In parenting the same principle applies.

Tweens need to know and understand the essential expectations their parents have of them. These include care of their pets and possessions, their personal hygiene, cleanliness of their bedroom and the common areas of their home and how they interact with each other in the family context. When I was a tween, manners were highly regarded. I was taught to say "please" and "thank you" and not to eat with my elbows on the table. Profanity was unacceptable in our home, and we spoke to each other and especially to adults with respectful language.

The expectations parents set for their tweens is critical in helping them become responsible now and into the future. These expectations need to be carefully thought-out and agreed on by the parents, and then clearly and carefully explained to the child.

Energy

Igniting and infusing the value of responsibility into the life of your tween will require energy—physical, intellectual, and emotional energy. It will take time and energy to establish the expectations you have of your tween in your home. It will also take energy to follow through and hold your tween accountable for the expectations required of them. Part of that accountability will involve consequences. This has been a huge area of discussion and debate among parenting experts over the years. How and when should parents discipline their children? What forms of discipline or consequences, if any, are effective in helping them become more responsible? Is discipline helpful or harmful in the long run?

The focus of this book is about developing your child's character by personally living and then leading them to live out certain values. It is not a guide that addresses all parenting issues with specific techniques. So, the only answer to the question of how to discipline a tween, or hold them accountable for their actions, involves three questions of my own for parents.

1. Do you have the emotional energy and stability to handle your tween's response to the consequences you deem necessary? In other words, do you care enough for them to not care about what they think of your decisions as a parent?

2. Is the goal of the discipline or consequences for your tween their long-term maturity, or is it just a short-term punishment? In other words, are the consequences going to benefit them in the long run and not just appease your anger or frustration for the wrongdoing?

3. Are you more concerned about the character of your tween or their behavior?

If you care too much about how your tween will react to the consequences and your focus is short-term punishment for their behavior, then no matter what consequences you choose, it will probably be a losing proposition. If you can emotionally handle any response from your tween to the consequences, and if your ultimate goal is to develop their maturity and character, then almost any consequences you choose will be appropriate. I think most parents' sense of awareness, judgment, insight, and wisdom are enough that they can choose consequences that are appropriate.

The other reality about consequences for irresponsibility is that they are often inevitable, even if no discipline is enacted; there are natural consequences for irresponsibility. One of the natural consequences of being irresponsible is that it breeds more irresponsibility.

Author Stephen R. Covey said, "While we are free to choose our actions, we are not free to choose the consequences of our actions." Josiah Stamp put it this way, "It is easy to dodge our responsibilities, but we cannot dodge the consequences of dodging our responsibilities."

Perhaps you have heard that responsibility means accepting the consequences for our actions. That is only partly true because sometimes we can dodge those immediate penalties. A twelve-year-old who shoplifts may not get caught and therefore may avoid the immediate consequences of their actions. The greater end to that story is that they might begin to believe that they can always avoid consequences for their actions. Responsibility also teaches us that when we do what is right, we will often (but not always) be rewarded for those actions. If I have a part-time job and I am punctual and work hard, I can expect to be paid, to keep the job, and possibly even to move ahead in the company. But if I show up late and don't perform my duties, I can expect negative outcomes.

One reward of responsibility is more responsibility. If you do what needs to be done, you will have learned responsibility. If you continue to live responsibly, you will become more attractive to employers, friends, and organizations because we all appreciate those who are responsible. Responsible people take care of themselves, their stuff, and their assignments, but infusing responsibility always requires energy.

Excellence

Responsibility also leads to excellence. When a tween begins to live with a sense of responsibility for themselves, their stuff, and their assignments, they begin to discover higher levels of achievement in many areas of their lives. When they are responsible in finishing their homework and assignments for school, practicing for band or athletics, and fulfilling their obligations at home or at a part-time job, they begin to experience a measure of success. A few people are born with very high levels of skill, talent, motivation, and competency that lead naturally to achievement. The rest of us have to work hard for it.

Excellence does not mean being perfect; rather it means being perfectly committed to doing one's best given the resources available at any given time. A tween who practices a musical instrument diligently, who attends band rehearsals consistently, and who is passionate about playing music will achieve a level of competence. That's what I call excellence. That means when they play in a school musical performance, they may not hit all the notes perfectly, but they will have done the best they could have done given the time they had to practice, the proficiency of the teaching, the quality of musical instrument available, and numerous other factors.

In the end, they will have performed with excellence, and that is certainly worthy of celebration.

Over the years I have had the privilege of leading several organizations, each with a large number of volunteers. There is something extraordinary about someone who chooses to invest their energy and talents into a project or people where there is no financial compensation for their efforts. I have always championed the value of excellence in every organization, meaning every volunteer should do their very best given the resources available to them at any given time. That understanding of excellence freed all the volunteers from the pressure to be perfect. We celebrated the best they could give and expected no more. Tweens should never be expected to be perfect, just perfectly committed to being the best they can be.

Ideas for igniting and infusing responsibility into your tween

- Ask yourself, on a scale of 1–10, how well does your tween take care of themselves, their stuff, and their assignments? How could they specifically step up their level of responsibility in those three areas?

- Talk to your tween about your first job. Describe the responsibilities and the expectations the job required, and what you enjoyed, dreaded, and learned from this job.

- Take a photo of your child on the first day of school each year and make sure to include a photo of their backpack to observe how both change.

- On each of their birthdays during their tween years, give them a gift that includes a measure of responsibility like a bicycle with a lock. Take the time to discuss the responsibilities associated with their gift.

Insights

- Responsibility is closely connected to maturity and means I will take care of myself, my stuff, and my assignments. The more responsible a person becomes, the more freedom they can enjoy.

- Parents must not over pack their tweens' lives with too much responsibility, but they must remind them there are loads they must carry on their own.

- Tweens should never be expected to be perfect, just perfectly committed to being the best they can be.

CHAPTER 6

COMMUNITY

"The key to the happy life, it seems, is the good life: a life with sustained relationships, challenging work, and connections to community."

– Paul Bloom

"I think that the path that I took was normal in the American society where young women and men are not trained as to how to make the transition from being a girl to being a woman, from being a boy to being a man. And so I think that most young people in America live by trial and error, and not by parental instruction or community guidance."

– Sister Souljah

Community: I will be a connected and contributing member of my tribe.

Tribe

At the time of writing this book, I have conducted over 2,400 life celebrations, including weddings, funerals and memorials, new life celebrations for babies, and coming-of-age ceremonies for thirteen-year-olds. Those who gather at these events are always connected to the individual, the couple, or their families that are being celebrated. This group of people includes immediate and extended family members, neighbors, coworkers, business associates, teammates, coffee or beer buddies, classmates, community members, and friends from various stages of life. I've never personally met a wedding (or funeral) crasher—someone who just shows up with no authentic connection. I think those people are only found in the movies.

These rites of passage are attended by people I call "the tribe." My simple definition of the tribe differs from many other people. I believe your tribe is defined as the friends and family members you can count on to be there for you when you need them the most. They will grieve with you in your darkest valley and cheer for you in your success on the mountaintop. One of the members of my tribe is my friend, David. When my mother, Alice, died at age fifty-nine, it never crossed my mind not to attend her funeral service. I was her son, part of her tribe. Of course I was there. And so were many others, including my friend David.

Several years after my mother's passing, I received the sad news that David's mother, Judy, had died. And it never crossed my mind to miss her funeral service either. When I received the news about her death and then the details about the memorial service, I immediately checked my schedule, not to see whether I could attend the service, but to see which appointments I would have to cancel because I was going to be there for David. That's what members of the tribe do. They come to you, they help you, they support you, and they love you, especially when you need them the most. They make sure you never have to stand alone, and that no one is left behind.

We have all heard the African proverb that it takes a village to raise a child. I believe differently. I would respectfully submit that regardless of whether or not a child has a village, what they really need is a tribe. I see the village as geographical, but the tribe as relational. My friend David lives in Florida; I live in Ontario. Despite the geographical distance between us, he has walked with me through my deepest darkness and celebrated with me in my greatest joy. He has always been there for me, for which I am eternally grateful. Every tween needs a tribe, a multigenerational group of family members and friends who will walk with them through their tween years. They need those who will love them unconditionally and provide a safe place for them to be accepted and to belong. Every tween needs a tribe.

Lego

When I was a child, I received a Lego set as a gift one Christmas. Lego is still very popular today, but it is very different from the set I received. Today, the Lego sets are high-tech and elaborate. They include movie or superhero characters, computer chips, and colorful backdrops. Back then, it was old school. It was just the building blocks. When I opened the container, I immediately spilled the Lego pieces on the floor and began to play with them. That began my childhood attachment with Lego. I loved to play with my Lego set. Alone or with friends, I used my imagination and built structures. I look back with much fondness on that special gift. Now, I don't play with Lego anymore, but there is one significant lesson I remember from my Lego days.

Just as the Lego pieces were different, people are different as well. We are different shapes, sizes, colors, backgrounds, and ages. But one thing we do share in common, however, is the need and the ability to connect with each other. Lego pieces are designed to connect, to fit together. Even though they are different, they still fit together beautifully. That's the way our tribe is. Parents, children, cousins, aunts, uncles, grandparents, stepparents, and close friends—we are all different, but somehow we all fit together. We belong together. The tribe does not have to be homogeneous or uniform. It is often an odd collection of people of different generations, genders, and cultures, proving there can be unity without uniformity. Tweens need exposure to people different from themselves in their tribe because at the end of the day, it's all about the connection.

Involved

Older tweens will begin the process of choosing their own members of their tribe. Like the teeter-totter example in their social development, they are moving away from parental influence to peer influence. They will add new friends to their community, and these friends may someday become more important to them than their own family members.

As a motorcyclist, I have attended several of the famous Friday the 13th bike events in Port Dover, Ontario. This gathering of motorcycle enthusiasts was started by Chris Simons on Friday, November 13, 1981. The celebration is attended by multitudes of people from all walks of life who share the common love for all things motorcycle. The spirit of community and camaraderie is as evident as their leather chaps and vests. People who don't know each other feel free to chat and enjoy the day together. Thousands of people share in this ritual, and they do so by getting together—you know, face-to-face and not just online. As great as social media and online connections can be, I believe there is something absolutely, wonderfully human about personal connection. It is sometimes awkward and challenging, but it is also healthy and necessary.

As busy as our lives can become, it is critical for parents to plan family reunions, vacations, holiday celebration get-togethers, birthday and graduation parties, rites-of-passage rituals, and other social gatherings for their tweens. These times of connection will create opportunities for your tween to get involved and have fun with their tribe. Fun. Yes, fun! Tribal gatherings should be fun. Music, dancing, food, decorations, games, conversation, inclusion, and laughter should all be part of these gatherings. We should look forward to our tribal gatherings. Life is hard, but it seems less so when we are in a supportive, committed community. Friday the 13th in Port Dover, Ontario, will always remind me how amazing it is just to go somewhere to hang out with people who share something in common. As fun as that event is, however, it is so much more extraordinary to hang out with my tribe.

Evolve

No tribe stays together and intact forever. Because relationships are made up of people and people are imperfect, there are no perfect relationships and no perfect tribes. The relationships in your tweenager's tribe will change over time. Sometimes members of their tribe will be become detached because of a relationship breakdown, a move away, a divorce, or even a death. Other times a member will be added to their tribe through the start of a new friendship, a marriage, or the birth of a new family member. New-life celebrations, birthdays, coming-of-age ceremonies, graduations, weddings, and funerals are rituals that have been traditionally celebrated by the tribe and community throughout history. When we get together for these events, we are mindful of those who are no longer part of the tribe and those who are newly added to it.

THE THIRTEENITIES

There will also be people that will join the tribe for a specific purpose and designated time frame. A teacher, coach, or tutor may be added to the tribe for a season, then they will step away. This evolution of the tribe is natural; however, it is important that your tween knows that there will always be those who are in the tribe for the long haul, regardless of the circumstances. Affirming your commitment as a parent to your child will help to provide a sense of emotional security for them at this emotionally unsteady time in their development. (Remember the roller-coaster illustration?)

Although some members of the tribe will already be chosen for your tween, they will begin to choose some members on their own. It is true: you can choose your friends but not your family. I encourage parents to be intentional in providing opportunities for their tween to connect with other tweens. You can never force friendships, but you can plan events where your tweens can meet new people and potentially establish new friendships. Summer camps, sports leagues, and youth groups are places where this can happen naturally.

Support

Author M. Scott Peck wrote, "There can be no vulnerability without risk; there can be no community without vulnerability; there can be no peace, and ultimately no life, without community." As a card-carrying member of the human race, I can affirm that failure is part of life. We try to avoid it, we cover it up, we minimize it, and we lie about it. The truth is that we all fail. We mess up, we misfire, we sin, we drop the ball, and we fall flat on our face. We all fail. Failure can be devastating for most people and even more so for tweens. Because of the social-media explosion on all platforms, gossip, photos, and videos can be shared instantly. This makes the fear of failure an even greater vulnerability for tweens.

One of the roles of the tribe is to be an accepting community, regardless of the level of success or failure of their members. I was once told that as a parent, there should be nothing bad my child could ever do to cause me to love them less or nothing great my child could ever do to cause me to love them more. My love, acceptance, and commitment to my children should never be based or their success or failure.

Throughout my tween years I experienced what I considered to be numerous colossal personal failures. In reality they really weren't that big of a deal, but to me, at that time in my life, they were. What I do remember, though, is that the support I received through the words and actions of those who loved me the most helped me through those times. A supportive conversation from my dad, a hug from my grandmother, a high five from my hockey coach—those were the simple things that reminded me that failure is just as much a part of life as is success, and that my value as a person was not measured by either. One of the roles of the tribe is to celebrate success, but also, with just as much energy and intention, to support tweens through times of failure. The tribe will remind your tween that failure is fertilizer from which good things can grow.

Ideas for igniting and infusing community into your tween

- As a parent (or parents), write down a list of those people you think might be part of your tween's tribe. Include family members, friends, and other significant adults. Once the list is completed, review it. Is it multigenerational? Are the influences on your tween positive, negative, or neutral? Are there others you think you could add to this list?

- Start to plan your tween's coming-of-age celebration. Read chapter 17 if you want to skip ahead. Who will you invite? When and where will it be?

THE THIRTEENITIES

- In a casual conversation, share with your tween one of the failures you experienced as a tween yourself. You don't have to share all the details; just be honest about what you felt at the time and how you managed to make it through the embarrassment of failure.

- When you were a tween, you probably had a few really close friends. If you haven't connected with them in a while, reach out and let them know you were thinking about them and that you appreciated their friendship.

Insights

- Community means that I will be a connected and contributing member of my tribe.

- I define a tribe as the friends and family members you can count on to be there for you when you need them the most. It is often an odd collection of people of different generations, genders, and cultures, proving there can be unity without uniformity.

- No tribe stays together and intact forever. Because relationships are made up of people and people are imperfect, there are no perfect relationships and no perfect tribes. Members of the tribe celebrate success and support tweens through times of failure.

CHAPTER 7

GENEROSITY

"Giving frees us from the familiar territory of our own needs by opening our mind to the unexplained worlds occupied by the needs of others."

– Barbara Bush

"All you have shall someday be given: Therefore give now, that the season of giving may be yours and not your inheritors."

– Kahlil Gibran

Generosity: I use what I have to help others in need.

Give

The tween that is moving toward greater maturity by demonstrating responsibility and a commitment to being a contributing member of their tribe will often have a desire to practically help others in need. This is the virtuous value of generosity, a value espoused by almost every religious and cultural group on Earth. Generosity means that one person uses what they have to help someone else who has a need. Generous people live with hearts open to express compassion, their eyes open to see the needs of those around them, and their hands open to serve and meet those needs in practical ways.

They may have money, a possession, time to volunteer, or a special skill or talent they can give away. Generosity says that the act of giving is best exercised when there is nothing expected in return—except perhaps for appreciation.

When I was a youth worker, I would organize service projects with different charitable agencies. One such agency was Ray of Hope in Waterloo Region, Ontario. They operated several facilities, one of which was a drop-in center. The center housed a soup kitchen, food and clothing banks, laundry facility, spiritual care staff, and numerous tutoring and educational support services for the poor and disenfranchised in our downtown core.

One evening I led a group of tweens and adult leaders to help out by providing a meal for the guests who were part of that community. After the meal was completed, the director took us on a tour of the entire facility. She told us all about the people they served and the difference they were making in our city's downtown core. She also told us about what they needed in order to operate effectively, including money, food, clothing, blankets, toiletries, and even bus tokens.

One attentive twelve-year-old boy quickly raised his hand and asked why they needed bus tokens. The director explained that even though the people they served didn't have cars or even bicycles, they still needed to get around the city for medical appointments, classes, or job interviews. Having bus tokens really helped them out. The young boy pulled about half a dozen tokens from his pocket and handed them to the director. "Here," he said, "I can ride my bike or walk to school this week. It sounds like these people need these more than I do." Now, I understand that the boy's parents probably bought the tokens for him, but I was still impressed with his spirit of generosity. He was willing to be responsible—he was still going to get to school on time—and help others by meeting a very specific need. The Hard Rock Café's motto is "Love all. Serve all." That's not a bad way to live.

Shopping

Parents can ignite and infuse the value of generosity into the lives of tweens in many ways. When one of my daughters was in her early tweens, we shared an experience that helped her understand the value and practical nature of being generous. I wish I could say this idea was planned out well in advance, but it wasn't.

As we went to our local grocery store one day, we both noticed a large box at the entrance, a square-shaped container used to collect food for our local food bank. Immediately, I thought it would be a good idea for us to donate some food. So I decided to do this: We would do our grocery shopping, but we would put all the grocery items we needed on one half of our shopping cart and an equal number of items for the food bank on the other half of the cart. It was a beautiful father-daughter experience as we talked about what we were buying for our family and what we were buying for another family in need. My daughter asked some very insightful questions: "Do you think they will have children my age? Do you think they eat spaghetti? What would they eat if we didn't buy something for them?" That shared, spontaneous experience of generosity was both meaningful and fun. I will never forget it.

Someone once told me you can do only three things with your money: you can save it, you can spend it, or you can give it away, and giving it away is always the most fun. Generous people find great joy in the simple act of giving. They know they can't help out everyone, but that doesn't stop them from helping someone. They have learned and live the adage: "Love people and use things. Not the other way around."

Serving

For tweens to become truly connected members of their tribe, they will need to begin to contribute to it. They will have to move from a mindset of getting to that of giving. This attitude flies directly in the face of the egocentric and self-centered pattern that floods the North American culture today. To set aside one's own agenda and resources to help someone else in need is a true mark of maturity and responsibility. Parents, you can begin now to infuse this value into the lives of your tweens.

When I was eleven years old, my parents asked me if I would be interested in helping out my great aunt Edna by cleaning her apartment. I was interested, so each Friday after school I would be dropped off at her place to begin the housework. I would vacuum, dust, and clean the bathroom. Her place was quite small, so it didn't take too long. The rest of the time was spent enjoying a simple dinner, watching some TV, or playing gin rummy. I look back with much fondness on those times, probably because I felt I was actually helping someone, and it felt really good. I was just using the ability to vacuum to help someone who was unable to do so.

After my great aunt passed away, my parents gave me a silver dollar that was part of her few possessions. Ironically, the coin was minted the year of my birth, and it is an heirloom I treasure to this day. I understand this much better now, but even though my great aunt Edna was over six decades older than me and we had very little in common, she was still part of my tribe. I was honored to serve this elderly woman by simply spending a few hours each week cleaning her apartment.

There will be a time in all our lives when the balance of energy and resources moves from the older to the younger. As parents, we benefit our tribe and the world as we model and instruct our children on the value of serving others in need. The good news is that I believe tweens are open to that vision of adulthood and will take steps toward it as parents infuse that value into their young lives.

Guilt

There are different means by which tweens are motivated to do (or not do) certain things. Some are motivated by external measures, which means they will change their behavior based on the promise of an external punishment or reward. Although this motivation may sometimes be effective in the short term, it rarely results in lasting behavioral change. Others may be motivated by internal incentives, which means they will do something because they really believe it to be true, good, or right. Again, this may have short-term results, and though it may be better than external motivation, I have some reservations about how effective this is for tweens. There are just too many unknowns about how they think and behave.

I raise this issue to remind parents of two considerations when it comes to motivating your tween toward generosity. The first is this: Parents, you cannot force your tween to be generous. Yes, you could come up with a plan to pay your children to donate to a charity, or perhaps punish them if they don't. But that undermines the entire meaning of generosity, doesn't it? Parents can provide opportunities and be a role model of generosity. They can discuss, affirm, and infuse generosity, but they can never force their children to truly be generous. That's a value they must personally embrace.

The second notion is this: parents should never use guilt as a motivator for their tween in the area of generosity or any of the other Thirteenities. Growing up in a conservative religious environment, I have an extensive understanding of how guilt can be used, misused, and abused. All I would say here is that parents should never manipulate their tweens by causing them to feel guilty about not embracing any of the Thirteenities, especially generosity. Guilt can be wrongly leveraged by parents when they compare their tweens to others, verbally put them down, or withhold any expected expression of their parental love. The value of generosity is too great to use guilt to force it on our tweens (or anyone else for that matter) or to manipulate them with guilt.

Wisdom

In the last chapter, we discovered that maturity and responsibility are best expressed in community and not in isolation. It is within the multigenerational tribe that tweens come to a better understanding of what it means to be mature and responsible. The same could be said of generosity. As tweens become more mature and responsible, they have a better chance of becoming a more generous individual. The other side of the coin is important as well. Generosity is best expressed in the context and foundation of maturity and responsibility. Unfortunately, tweens that flourish in generosity are at risk of being taken advantage of and need protection from those that would do them harm. Again, this is where parents specifically and the tribe generally can provide wisdom.

Each can appropriately inform the tween about how to manage their schedule and finances so that they can donate from a surplus position. They can help tweens decide whether or not a cause or individual is the best recipient of their generosity. Most importantly though, the tribe can help a tween live the value of generosity in a responsible manner. The advice and role modeling—particularly of older members of their tribe— can help tweens learn how and where to be generous.

They can also practically meet the needs of others by serving together. The opportunities to serve members of our tribe and others are numerous, from practical work projects, to emotional support through visits and spending time, to sending words of support to those who are sick or in special physical need. These service projects can be done individually or in groups. They can be planned or spontaneous, big or small. The obvious outcome will be tweens who will understand that being an adult carries with it the responsibility to serve others, starting with those closest to them first.

Ideas for igniting and infusing generosity into your tween

- Plan a family or multiple family service project—collect food for the food bank, do a "rake and run" where you rake leaves in the autumn at the home of a senior citizen or someone who is physically unable to do so. If you live in a wintery climate, you could also do a "shovel and split" (I'm sure you can figure that one out on your own).

- Regularly discuss time and financial management with your tween. Include the three things you can do with money: save it, spend it, or give it away.

- If your tween receives an allowance or gets paid for work they do, you can help them create a budget and explain how wise financial management can allow them to serve and give to others in need.

- As a parent (or parents), evaluate or discuss this quote from C.S. Lewis: "I do not believe one can settle how much we ought to give. I am afraid the only safe rule is to give more than we can spare. In other words, if our expenditure on comforts, luxuries, amusements, etc., is up to the standard common among those with the same income as our own, we are probably giving away too little. If our charities do not at all pinch or hamper us, I should say they are too small. There ought to be things we should like to do and cannot do because our charitable expenditures excludes them."

Insights

- Generosity means that I use what I have to help others in need.

- Generous people find great joy in the simple act of giving. They know they can't help out everyone, but that doesn't stop them from helping someone.

- Parents benefit their tribe and the world as they model and instruct their children on the value of serving others in need. They can never force their children to truly be generous, and should never use guilt as a motivator. The tribe can help a tween live the value of generosity in a responsible manner.

CHAPTER 8

HUMILITY

"There is a universal respect and even admiration for those who are humble and simple by nature, and who have absolute confidence in all human beings irrespective of their social status."

– Nelson Mandela

"Stay hungry, stay young, stay foolish, stay curious, and above all, stay humble because just when you think you got all the answers, is the moment when some bitter twist of fate in the universe will remind you that you very much don't."

– Tom Hiddleston

Humility: I will cultivate an attitude of thankfulness.

Success

Every parent wants their tween to succeed in life. The challenge for many parents is defining what they mean by "success." Often what success means to a parent comes in the form of a dream or vision they have for their child. They dream of their child growing up to eventually enjoy a lucrative career, respect in the community, a happy marriage, and good children. Some parents even live vicariously through their kids. They want their children to accomplish what they didn't. Then they find a sense of deep, but fraudulent, personal gratification through their children's success. I have observed that people often define success by looking through one of three lenses: the lens of the culture, the tribe, and that which is self-defined.

The culture defines success mostly through the media, entertainment, and advertising. We see images of sexy bodies, wealth and possessions, designer fashions, confidence, achievements, and individualism. The culture seems to celebrate that brand of success, even if it is just a disguise. The self-defined meaning of success can be a bit problematic as well as it can be easily altered by the individual when their circumstances change.

I prefer for success to be framed by the tribe of a tweenager. What I mean is that the multigenerational voices of the tribe can help a tween understand and pursue success based on those who know them best. When I was a tween, I had members of my tribe, especially coaches and teachers that I respected, who told me I could and should be doing better and achieving more. I also had those who reminded me that developing my character was just as important as improving my slap shot, and respecting myself and others was more important than receiving applause from the crowd. The wisdom and counsel of my tribe was valuable, and I am humbled and grateful for those who helped me understand what success really was.

Shoulders

At a conference I attended many years ago, one of the speakers challenged us to complete an interesting exercise. We were asked to think back over our childhood years and to identify the significant adults we felt had a meaningful influence on us as we were growing up. The purpose of the exercise was for each of us to better understand the large number of individuals who helped us become what we are today. It was actually after the conference that I accepted the challenge, but with a specific focus. I sat down with a pen and piece of paper and began to write the names of significant adults that influenced my life up until I was thirteen years old. Here were my findings:

- two parents

- four grandparents

- thirty teachers from grades kindergarten to eight

- fourteen sports coaches, instructors, club leaders, tutors, Sunday school teachers, youth workers, counselors, extended family members, and good neighbors

Now, I understand that my recollection of the exact numbers may be a bit off and that each adult did not provide the same level of influence on my life. That said, I was surprised to discover that the total number was fifty. There were fifty significant adults who played a part in my personal growth and development up until the end of my tween years. That discovery was both thrilling and humbling. Some of these people have passed away. I have lost contact with many others. Some knew they were meaningfully shaping my life. Others were unaware. The point is that I owe each of them a substantial debt of gratitude for what they did for me. Some were paid professionals. Others were organizational volunteers. Many were just individuals who were important to me without title or formal position.

It is on those shoulders (and the shoulders of many others) that I stand today. Who I am, what I have learned about life, and the expression of my character were all shaped in those formative years. Who our children are and who they are becoming is unquestionably influenced by the population of significant role models on whose shoulders they someday will stand. That understanding, which may not come until they are well into their adult years, will eventually lead our children to a sentiment of humble gratitude.

Assist

Infusing the value of humility into the lives of tweens will be just as difficult as it is important. Humility is a mysterious attribute because if you say that you have attained a measure of it, you lose a bit of it at the same time. It is also difficult to define, but you sure know it when you see it. I think humility is confidence without arrogance, pride in one's personal accomplishments and equal pride in the achievements of others, and graciousness in both victory and in defeat. Humility is giving honor and respect where it is due. It is acknowledging that even the most brilliant among us still does not know everything about everything. It is striving for greatness, but also assisting others in their struggle to achieve greatness as well.

I love humble people, especially the great ones. I live less than an hour away from where one of the greatest hockey players was born. Wayne Gretzky from Brantford, Ontario, earned the nickname, "The Great One." If you follow hockey, I don't need to remind you of the extraordinary success he achieved in his twenty-year professional career. When he retired in 1999, he held an incredible sixty-one NHL records. One of his records that remains (at the time of the writing of this book) is being the all-time assist leader. In 1,487 games he scored 894 goals, but he assisted on 1,963 goals—an unbelievable 1.32 assists-per-game average over the span of his career. In other words, he helped his teammates score twice as many goals as he scored himself. In addition to being a classy player, his body of work reminds me that part of being truly successful involves assisting others to be successful as well.

We should be teaching our tweens to be great, and that humility reminds us to be thankful instead of boastful. Or, as I have often said, "Be great. But in being great, always be grateful."

Vertigo

I will never forget my fortieth birthday. I was really looking forward to a few days off and had a short trip planned. Two days before I was to leave, I was in a leadership team meeting. Suddenly and without any warning, I became severely dizzy and nauseous. I made my way to the washroom and tried to regain my composure, but it was not to be. Shortly after, I was taken to the hospital, and following numerous tests, the doctor revealed that I had benign positional vertigo. BPV is caused when there is a disruption in the semicircular canals or the tubes in your inner ear. This causes dizziness, blurred vision, and loss of balance. Basically you look like a drunken toddler wearing a blindfold. It was a horrible experience. The good news is that with medication and about a week's rest, I was back to normal.

What I will never forget about that event is the fear that gripped me when I couldn't even stand up because of the dizziness. For a few brief moments, I was terrified of having things taken from me, like my ability to provide for my family, to play with my children, or to enjoy playing hockey or riding my motorcycle. It was a humbling experience, to say the least.

Humility is a good thing, but sometimes it is best learned when life becomes bad. It causes us to pause and often gives us a fresh perspective. Occasionally when I am on a motorcycle, I will recall my fortieth birthday and the lesson I learned— that life itself has a way of igniting humility in our lives. In his book *The Little Minister*, James Matthew Barrie reminds us all that, "Life is a long lesson in humility."

Thanks

Parents should never degrade their children; that's humiliation, not humility. Parents can help their tweens understand that humility is achieving success without defeating or destroying other people. It is a value that accepts that failure and mistakes are part of life and should be understood as steps in the process of growing. It reminds us that our knowledge is limited, that the universe is a very big place, and that none of us is at the center of it. We all have our faults and imperfections, but that is not reason enough to stop striving for greatness and goodness in life. Humility declares equally be great and be grateful because all we have can be lost in a single moment.

Humility honors those who sacrificed in the past so that we can enjoy the present. It appreciates all the gifts life brings. Humility is a natural expression of maturity and responsibility. Tweens that are growing in responsibility will express that through the values of community, generosity, and humility specifically by gathering with their tribe, giving to those in need, and expressing gratitude.

Ideas for igniting and infusing humility into your tween

- Take a few minutes before a meal and have each family member share something for which they are thankful.

- Share with your tween a mistake you made or a painful failure that you experienced when you were their age, and let them know what things you learned from that and how that helped you in the long run.

- Write a "just because" thank-you note to your tween, expressing appreciation for some quality you see developing in them. Leave it in a place they will find it.

- Take some time to identify those people who really influenced your life up until you were age thirteen. Compile a written list and express gratitude for each of these individuals.

Insights

- Humility means I will cultivate an attitude of thankfulness.

- Who our children are and who they are becoming is unquestionably influenced by the population of significant role models on whose shoulders they someday will stand. That understanding, which may not come until they are well into their adult years, will eventually lead our children to a sentiment of humble gratitude.

- Parents should never degrade their children; that's humiliation, not humility. We should be teaching our tweens to be great, and that humility reminds us to be thankful instead of boastful. In other words, "Be great. But in being great, always be grateful."

CHAPTER 9

INTEGRITY

"Live so that when your children think of fairness and integrity, they think of you."
– H. Jackson Brown Jr.

"A life lived with integrity—even if it lacks the trappings of fame and fortune—is a shining star in whose light others may follow in the years to come."
– Denis Waitley

Integrity: I will say and do what is right and honorable.

Wheel

Just north of the twin cities of Kitchener-Waterloo, Ontario where I grew up, is Mennonite country. For many Mennonites, the means of transportation is still the horse and buggy. The wheels on those buggies or wagons are handmade of wood and steel with a center hub, the wheel itself, and numerous spokes connecting those two parts. The craftsmanship is extraordinary. These wheels are handmade with great care so that they are both strong and durable. After they are built, tested, and ready to be used, they are said to have structural integrity. That means they are whole, unbroken, and complete.

The virtuous value of integrity carries a similar meaning. A person of integrity lives their life with completeness and congruency. They speak and act the same way in every area of their life, and what they say and do flows naturally from their core beliefs. For example, there are many people that say they believe that being honest is very important, regardless of the consequences. Some of those people live with that belief in a complete and congruent way and are honest at all times, with all people, in every situation. Then there are others who are often honest, but not always with all people in every situation. They embrace honesty, but they do not have the integrity to embrace it in every situation.

Integrity is the strength needed to live your core beliefs in every area of your life. Like a sturdy wagon wheel, those with integrity move forward in their lives with alignment between their beliefs and their behaviors.

Trivia

Another "wheel" illustration I often use in my keynote speaking is the wheel pattern on a Trivial Pursuit game board. The game was created by two Canadian men, Chris Haney and Scott Abbott, and was released in 1982. The game board has the shape of a wagon wheel printed on it. There is a central hub, an outside wheel, and spokes connecting those two parts. Where each of the six spokes connect with the outside wheel are specific categories, which differ depending on the version of the game.

I believe that integrity means that your core beliefs are expressed consistently in all the categories of your life. The hub, or heart, of your life should affect every category of it as well. I am not convinced that integrity builds your beliefs or worldview; it just ensures they are lived out harmoniously in all areas of your life. And even though integrity is a virtuous value, it does not guarantee a virtuous life by itself. Someone with immoral or evil values can still be a person of integrity as long as they act consistently on those beliefs. Adolf Hitler and Mother Teresa both lived with integrity, despite the fact their core beliefs varied greatly.

I discuss the subject of core beliefs in other chapters of *The Thirteenities*, specifically purity and spirituality. Tweens despise hypocrisy and duplicity but are attracted to people who know what they believe, and who live so that their beliefs and actions are in alignment—perhaps not perfectly, but not pretentiously either. Inspiring your tween to live with integrity is an ongoing mission for parents.

Donuts

True integrity always exposes our true character. The character of a tween includes all the moral attributes that make them who they really are. Good character qualities might include traits like punctuality, loyalty, self-restraint, patience, or confidence. These qualities are most often revealed when life is tough, not when it is stress-free.

A friend of mine was teaching this lesson to some young adolescents, and he illustrated it in a fun, memorable way. He set several jelly-filled donuts on a table and invited the students to try to guess the different filling in each donut. The students examined and smelled them. They argued and debated. But they could not come to full agreement as to what filling was in each donut. My friend informed the students that there was one sure way they could know what the filings were. He picked one up and with his bare hand, he squished it. All of a sudden, blueberry filling dripped down his arm and onto the floor. The smell of blueberry filled the room. Obviously it was a blueberry-jelly-filled donut—or at least it once was. He concluded the lesson remarking that, like the donuts, people often look similar from the outside. Their real character, however, is only truly revealed when life squeezes them with illness, financial pressure, or some other kind of pressure or stress. That's when you really know who they are.

Parents, when your tween's life gets tough, you will discover their character. More important than that, when life gets tough for you, they will discover yours.

Promise

Living as a person with integrity means that we are honest and sincere and that we keep our promises. Being a parent of a tween is hard work. Sometimes, in the fast-paced flow of family life, parents make hasty promises to their children that end up unfulfilled. Some parents will even intentionally make a promise to their child they know they will not keep just to end an argument or to pacify them. The value of integrity forces parents to be more careful with their words. It also influences parents to clearly communicate the difference between an idea (I heard there's a new ice cream shop in the neighborhood. Wouldn't it be great to go there some time to check it out?) and a promise (I heard there's a new ice cream shop in the neighborhood. I will take you there this weekend to check it out). Ideas can and should be shared freely, but they remain only ideas until there is a commitment associated with them; the idea then becomes a promise. Integrity means we keep our promises even if the circumstances under which you made that promise changed.

Honesty

When I ask parents of tweens what values they want to see in their children, "honesty" is often their first response. There is something about honesty that is universally respected, maybe because it is so rare. Honesty has more to do with living honorably than just speaking the truth although the two ideas are closely connected because the person who speaks truthfully lives honorably and vice versa. Honest people don't find it necessary to embellish and exaggerate the truth.

They find no reason to tell only part of the truth or to put a spin on it so that it doesn't reflect poorly on them. Honesty is genuine, not deceptive. The tween who lives with integrity will say and do what is right and honorable, often because they have seen it modeled by their parents.

Ideas for igniting and infusing integrity into your tween

- Play a game of Trivial Pursuit with your tween and explain to them the image of the wagon wheel as it relates to integrity.

- Ask your tween who they think is the most honest person they know. Ask why they think there are not more honest people in the world.

- Give your tween permission to be totally honest with you, regardless of how either of you feels, or what consequences may result.

- Try the donut illustration with your tween. Have paper towels close by to clean up the mess.

Insights

- Integrity means I will say and do what is right and honorable.

- Like a sturdy wagon wheel, those with integrity move forward in their lives with alignment between their beliefs and their behaviors. Tweens despise hypocrisy and duplicity but are attracted to people who know what they believe, and who live so that their beliefs and actions are in alignment.

- When your tween's life gets tough, you will discover their character. More important than that, when life gets tough for you, they will discover yours. Integrity means we keep our promises even if the circumstances under which you made that promise changed.

CHAPTER 10

PURITY

*"I will not let anyone walk through
my mind with their dirty feet."*

– Gandhi

*"When a man has so far corrupted and prostituted
the chastity of his mind, as to [profess] things
he does not believe, he has prepared himself
for the commission of every other crime."*

– Thomas Paine

Purity: I will fill my mind with what is true and wholesome.

Water

One thing we in North America often take for granted is the accessibility of clean drinking water. Just turn on your tap and there it is. Now, when I say "clean drinking water," I don't mean it is totally free from contaminates, but it is generally safe for human consumption. I had the chance to attend a

Children's Groundwater Festival with my son on a school trip when he was in grade five (in the middle of his tweendom). The event was both fascinating and informative and reminded me that water is the basis for life and clean water is essential for good health. Contaminated water brings disease and sometimes death. I learned about the natural water cycle, which is powered by gravity, and how the sun converts contaminated water into pure water. All of this reminds me of the virtuous value of purity. We all know it is best to drink water free from contaminates. I believe it is also best to take in what is true and wholesome in every area of our lives. Just like impure water can cause physical health problems, so taking in impure messages and thoughts is also unhealthy. Purity, along with tenacity and flexibility, is the offspring of integrity.

Mind

Purity is a moral virtue that begins in the mind. Although tweens need to be taught the importance of cleanliness and personal hygiene for their bodies, they also should learn about purity in their thinking patterns. This means keeping their minds unpolluted from that which would bring harm and lead them to negative behaviors. For instance, if a child is constantly exposed to non-consequential violence through video games, movies, and TV programming, their mind is being programmed to believe that violence is a viable solution to personal and relational conflict. That does not automatically indicate that the child will behave with physical violence when faced with relational conflict. However, my many years of experience working with young people would suggest that it does increase that possibility for some. Tweens, like everyone else, make decisions based on their value system and what they believe to be true. The mind is like the hub of a wagon wheel. All areas of our life, all decisions we make, and all actions we perform are a result of what we believe in our mind. Our thoughts influence our behavior in every area of our lives. Peer pressure, education, life experience, family structure, and maturity all play roles in this, but the constant bombardment of any message into a tween's brain will eventually have some impact on their behavior.

Discern

Parents can help their tweens begin to discern between what is helpful and what is harmful in their thinking patterns. I believe this discernment begins with dialogue—and often dialogue about thought-provoking and potentially embarrassing issues. The list of these issues seems to increase every week, and tweens are often exposed to them with very little mature guidance to help them navigate through them and to be able to understand their complexity. Life can be very confusing at times. It takes the confident leadership of a parent to invite their tween into open, candid conversations about anything, including self-worth, sexuality, addictions, depression, suicide, violence, fear, and anxiety. Part of that leadership includes dialogue to discover and reveal truth. Often these opportunities are spontaneous, so parents need to be ready at any time to have an open and accepting conversation with their tween.

Truth

A colleague and friend of mine named Tim used a phrase in a training seminar that I will always remember: "The truth will often hurt, but it never harms." He would then explain that telling someone the truth may bring them some short-term hurt, like hurt feelings. But telling the truth would always help, not harm them, in the long run. Water becomes pure and healthy when any contaminates are filtered out. When a parent lovingly speaks truth to their tween, it may cause hurt, but never harm. And eventually, just like pure water is clear, a tween who understands the truth about life will have a mind that is more clearly focused on what decisions to make and what direction they should go. Purity helps to unclutter our minds and discern the hurtful from the helpful.

Simple

We often associate purity with religious rituals or sexual chastity. Although I believe eleven-year-olds are too young emotionally to be sexually active, the concept of purity encompasses so much more. Purity is a mindset that leads to a lifestyle. For instance, I agree with the concept of free speech; however, that does not mean I have to tolerate someone who uses that freedom to pollute my mind with language that is crude, vulgar, or obscene. I have worked in some jobs where I felt I needed a mental detox after work just to clear my head of all the profanity to which I was exposed. I think profanity has its place—after all, I am a fan of the Toronto Maple Leafs. I just do not think it needs to be included in every sentence someone speaks. Purity informs tweens of simple truths. The world is full of both truth and lies, and we need to learn to discern between them. No one is without their faults and shortcomings. Even though the world is filled with suffering and injustice, life itself is beautiful and precious. True happiness is not found in the accumulation of possessions, but in the simplicity of contentment, the striving for betterment, and in serving others in need. It is an honor and responsibility for parents to ignite and infuse messages of purity into their tweens.

Ideas for igniting and infusing purity into your tween

- Remind your tween that although profanity is not appropriate in everyday language, it does happen. Both of you will need to agree to acknowledge that it does happens, that it is not acceptable, and that you each desire to clean up your own potty mouth.

- As a parent (or parents), take some time to assess the messages that your tween is exposed to through social media, entertainment, and advertising. How would you evaluate these messages in terms of the virtuous values you wish your tween to embrace?

- Compile a list of topics you think that you and your tween will probably have a discussion about someday. Use that list as a guide to help you better understand the issues, before you have the conversation.

- Create times for you and your tween to be in nature. Go camping, hiking, or kayaking. Get as unplugged as possible. Spending time in nature helps to clear our minds from the mental clutter and pollution we often are exposed to. Plus, it's really fun.

Insights

- Purity means I will fill my mind with what is true and wholesome.

- Just like impure water can cause physical health problems, so taking in impure messages and thoughts is also unhealthy. Purity is a moral virtue that begins in the mind. Our thoughts influence our behavior in every area of our lives. The constant bombardment of any message into a tween's brain will eventually have some impact on their behavior

- Parents can help their tweens begin to discern between what is helpful and what is harmful in their thinking patterns. It begins dialogue often about thought-provoking and potentially embarrassing issues. "The truth will often hurt, but it never harms."

CHAPTER 11

TENACITY

*"The most difficult thing is the decision
to act, the rest is merely tenacity."*

– Amelia Earhart

*"Nothing in the world can take the place of persistence.
Talent will not; nothing is more common than
unsuccessful individuals with talent. Genius will not;
unrewarded genius is almost a proverb. Education will
not; the world is full of educated derelicts.
Persistence and determination alone are omnipotent."*

– Ray Kroc

Tenacity: I will not give up or give in.

Name tag

Tenacity wears many name tags: determination, stick-to-itiveness, persistence, perseverance. It is that universally enviable character quality that declares that everyone will have to be persistent in order to accomplish their goals. It embodies hard work, mental toughness, practice, overcoming obstacles, and an unwavering commitment to see a vision become reality. Motivation and inspiration are often what you need to start, but tenacity is required in order to finish. "Tenacity" is often a word championed by entrepreneurs or athletes. They would say it is what they needed to create a company, design an innovative product or service, or win a championship. However, the word is not theirs exclusively. "Tenacity" is a word anyone can own because it is required to learn a new language, recover from an injury, pass an exam, overcome injustice, beat addiction, or make it through any hardship or challenge life throws at you. I love this word. I love how it sounds. I love what it means. I love when tweens experience it as well.

Hockey

I learned about tenacity when I played minor hockey as a child. Hockey has always been part of my life. As a typical Canadian kid growing up in the sixties and seventies with a dad and three brothers, I played a lot of hockey. I played on schoolyard rinks, ponds, in gyms, and in arenas. Our home backed on to a schoolyard, and my dad would flood a rink there each winter. On Saturdays, my brothers and I would play hockey all day, only taking breaks for lunch and to use the washrooms. I played minor hockey in Kitchener until I had a growth spurt when I was thirteen, then I turned my attention to basketball. After college, I returned to playing pickup hockey wherever I lived.

When I think back on my childhood, I remember my hockey coach's words of wisdom. After a loss, he said something like this:

> Boys, in this game you will lose as many times as you will win. Either way, when you leave this room and the door hits your butt on the way out,

the game is over. The key is to learn not only how to celebrate the victories, but to learn from the losses and be better prepared to play the next game. In hockey, it is not how big you are. It is not how strong you are. It is not even how skilled you are, or how well you are coached. It is always about how tough you are. It is about how big your heart is. It is about respecting yourself, your teammates and coaches, the referees, and even your opponents. In hockey, it is often the team with the most tenacity who wins. So we all walk out of this room with our heads up.

Tenacity often wins the day. In life, there will always be others who are smarter or stronger. There will always be challenges and obstacles that seem insurmountable. There will always be those who will criticize and oppose your dreams or your beliefs. Tweens need to learn tenacity as they will face numerous obstacles throughout their lives.

Bus

Tenacity is connected to integrity because it requires mental and emotional toughness to do what is right and honorable in a culture that doesn't necessarily embrace either of those values. The actions of Mrs. Rosa Parks remind me of the value of tenacity. Rosa was a forty-two-year-old African American woman who lived in Montgomery, Alabama. Every day she would take the bus to and from her job as a seamstress. In the 1950's every city bus in Montgomery was segregated. The front ten seats were reserved for white people, the last rows were for those who were black. On December 1, 1955, Rosa found herself sitting just behind the tenth row. Soon all the seats on the bus were filled. A short time later, a white man got on the bus and, finding it full, insisted that the four black people sitting in the row that Rosa found herself, give up their seat so he could sit there. Mrs. Parks quietly refused. Her action was not premeditated, but rather based in her firm belief in equality, personal rights, and justice. She later said, "When I made that decision, I knew that I had the strength of my ancestors with me." Her decision has forever marked her in American history as an influence in the civil rights movement.

I believe Rosa Parks demonstrated what it means to be tenacious. She did what was right and honorable in the face of opposition and injustice. She stood against bigotry, while the cultural norm allowed it. Tenacity is needed to intentionally act and spontaneously respond to situations that might otherwise cause someone to give up or give in. Tenacity is a virtuous value that can and should be ignited and infused into the lives of tweens.

Steps

It takes tenacity to reach your goals, unless your goal is to be a lazy, unproductive member of society. No tenacity is required for that. For all other goals, it is a requirement. The idea of goal setting is important for tweens because it helps them to learn patience, focus, and delayed gratification. More important than goals are the specific steps required to reach a goal.

I have set numerous goals in my own life. The ones I have reached always had a plan, a system, a road map, or steps to accomplishing it. When I lost fifty pounds of body weight in 2015, I didn't lose fifty pounds all at one time; I lost one pound, fifty times. Each day I went to the gym, or shopping for groceries, or planning my daily schedule was a step toward that goal. Every day it was a battle for me, and it still is. I have discovered that it is the small, regular, habitual, steps toward a goal that will bring success. When it comes to my goals, I have replaced the words "instant" and "immediate" with "journey" and "progress," and ultimately "success." Tweens need to learn patience and tenacity when it comes to achieving their goals.

Fail

I could (and may) write an entire book on failure. I have experienced failure in my own life in many areas—relationships, finances, business, and health. There are times that I feel that I have failed more than I have succeeded. However, the biggest lesson I have learned about failure is this: failure is only really failure if you fail to learn from failure.

One hard but necessary thing about parenting is watching your preadolescent children fail. A good parent would never cause their child to fail but will allow it to happen because they understand that the greatest life lessons are best learned in the valleys, not on the mountaintop. Walking with your tween through times of failure will affirm that they are always loved—not just when they succeed. It will teach them that they will probably fail in as many ventures as they will succeed. It will also strengthen their mindset to know that failure is not fatal or final or foreign because we all experience it.

I was fascinated to read an article about hockey goalie coach David Marcoux and the five Rs he teaches goalies to do after being scored on: release, relax, review, regroup, and refocus. Someone once told me that a hockey goalie has the hardest job in the world because when they make a mistake, a horn sounds, a red light goes off, and 20,000 people boo (or cheer, depending on whether the game is played at home or on the road).

Sometimes when your tween makes a mistake, they feel like a goalie who has just been scored on. Learning to recover from failure is one of life's greatest lessons, and parents can be the ones to teach this to your tweens.

Ideas for igniting and infusing tenacity in your tween

- Watch a movie with your tween about someone coming back after a major setback. Talk about the value of tenacity.

- There are many posters that speak to the value of tenacity and determination; often these include a quote from someone famous. Buy one for your tween and give it to them as a "just because" gift.

- Talk to your tween about failure and remind them that it will happen; however, let them know to learn from it and move forward as a better person. When they are in the middle of a failure, no talk is necessary, just some ice cream and a hug.

- Discuss goal setting and the importance of taking steps toward a goal with your tween. Ask your tween to share a few goals they might have and offer assistance in taking steps toward that goal.

Insights

- Tenacity means I will not give up or give in.

- It is that universally enviable character quality that declares that everyone will have to be persistent in order to accomplish their goals. Tenacity is needed to intentionally act and spontaneously respond to situations that might otherwise cause someone to give up or give in.

- Tweens need to learn patience and tenacity when it comes to achieving their goals. Sometimes when your tween makes a mistake, they feel like a goalie who has just been scored on. Learning to recover from failure is one of life's greatest lessons, and parents can be the ones to teach this to your tweens.

CHAPTER 12

FLEXIBILITY

"Have the capacity to adapt to change, it's your healthy growth, intelligently and emotionally. Our life can be full of extrinsic surprises,
your flexibility is a key when you accept changes."

– Angelica Hopes

"There can be no life without change, and to be afraid of what is different or unfamiliar is to be afraid of life."

– Theodore Roosevelt

Flexibility: I will adapt to change.

Dreams

Children daydream about what they will do or be when they grow up. These dreams start at a young age and are usually quite fanciful. They want to be a princess, astronaut, or professional athlete. As they grow older, those dreams change. The realities of life trump the fantasy of their childhood dreams. That doesn't mean they should give up their dreams or give up dreaming. On the contrary, dreams are what lead us to imagine what the future could be. Flexibility in the life of a tween is the ability to recalibrate their dreams to align better with who they really are.

I grew up with many boys who had a dream of making the NHL and becoming professional hockey players. I know only a few of them who actually made it. Statically, the chances are very low. However, many of them still play the game they love recreationally and have achieved success in other arenas of life. Their original dream was not realized, but another dream has been.

The wisdom of the tribe is most valuable in helping tweens adjust their dreams without destroying their passion. Tweens need to speak with and hear the stories of their grandparents, aunts and uncles, older cousins, and peers of their parents when it comes to pursing their dreams. They need to be introduced to individuals who have succeeded in the career they think they may want to pursue. They need to meet musicians, businesspeople, authors, makeup artists, software developers, retail managers, health care professionals, and athletes. This pool of experience and wisdom will help tweens start to dream with a better sense of reality.

Dreaming with reality—now that's an oxymoron, isn't it? But that's how flexibility operates. It invites wisdom and maturity to modify the childishness and foolishness of dreams, making them a true vision of a preferred future, making them dreams worthy of pursuit and passion.

106

The accelerating amount of change in our world creates an increasing amount of stress for those who lack flexibility. Changes that are forced on us require us to learn new ways of navigating our way through life. Changes in work policies, school expectations, and municipal laws, as well as the extensive changes in products and services being offered in the marketplace can be overwhelming. It is difficult to keep up with everything that has changed. Flexibility invites us into a lifestyle of continued growth and learning to adjust to changes that are happening. It is an attitude and a mindset. As we get older, this becomes more of a challenge. When we have become accustomed to operating our lives in a certain way, we experience a certain level of comfort. When changes come, we become emotionally uncomfortable. Flexibility opens our minds to adapting to new realities without compromising our integrity.

Several years ago, I conducted a funeral service for a man named Gordon who was born in October 1905 and died in May of 2012. He lived 106 years on Earth, and he is the oldest person for whom I have lead a funeral service. Gordon was a remarkable man. He was married seventy-seven years to his dear wife, Evelyn (who died at age 101). He worked for the Firestone Rubber Company as a mechanical engineer and helped develop better safety measures in tires that were implemented worldwide. He loved to golf, fish, invest in stocks, and dance. He was intelligent, stubborn, resourceful, and passionate. For his ninetieth birthday, his family bought him a laptop computer. Gordon never had a laptop before; he never needed one. But the world had changed. Now, Gordon could have left the laptop in its box and remained in his comfortable non-laptop world, but that wasn't his style. He knew the world had changed, and he wanted to change with it. So he tucked the laptop under his arm and took a bus (he couldn't drive) to a computer store. He set the laptop on the counter and asked the heavily tattooed young associate if he could teach him how to use it. The associate agreed and that was the beginning of a new world of enjoyment and learning for Gordon.

As I think about Gordon, I appreciate his commitment to the value of flexibility. Change comes to everyone, but those with a mindset of flexibility will navigate through life more successfully.

Strike

In the early 1990s, I had the responsibility of running big events for teenagers from across Ontario as a denominational youth director. One event that my team and I ran for years was called "See You at the Dome." We would purchase thousands of tickets for students to come to SkyDome in Toronto to watch a basketball or baseball game, then listen to inspirational talks given by several pro athletes.

In the late fall of 1993, we began to prepare for our 1994 calendar of events. Our promotion for SYATD September 1994 had begun. We had secured several thousand tickets for a Toronto Blue Jays game and were looking forward to an amazing event. Our plans continued to progress through the summer, and everything was on target. Then the unthinkable happened: on August 12, 1994, the Major League Baseball players went on strike. The game was cancelled, and the players were now unable to participate at our event. It was a major league disappointment (excuse the pun). We had invested thousands of dollars and hundreds of hours of time into this event already. It was so discouraging.

I met with my executive leadership team to discuss our options. We knew we could just write it off, or we could create a different event on the same day we had originally scheduled. I'm so glad to say that my team understood the value of flexibility, and we charged ahead—with a slightly different plan. We made some calls and rented the SkyDome, and SYATD 1994 became a reality. It ended up being one of the best events we had ever run.

Instead of watching a baseball game from the stands, our students got to play baseball on the field. Over two thousand young people played large group games, enjoyed music and food, and listened to several keynote speakers from the Canadian Football League. I will never forget it. I learned that year that success in life requires a commitment to flexibility. Tweens can understand that lesson as well.

Fear

Flexibility is a value that is expressed in reaction to something that has changed or is changing. Curiosity, which we will discover in a few chapters, is a value that is proactive in learning that results in personal growth and change. The biggest challenge to embracing flexibility is fear. We are afraid of the unknown and uncomfortable with the prospect of change. We also fear that maybe our assumptions about life may not be entirely accurate.

Tweens will respond differently to changes that are beyond their control. Some will become anxious and withdraw, others will greet the changes with enthusiasm as they accept the change as a new challenge. It is understandably difficult for many tweens to have to deal with big changes like divorce, death, moving to a new city, or starting at a new school. Parents need to understand the personalities of their tweens and help them navigate through the changes they are facing. They can help keep their home life simple, scheduled, and structured for their tweens and have reasonable expectations of them during times of transition.

Open

Flexibility is also required as tweens are exposed to new information and have to adapt to new ways of understanding the world. The news that Santa Claus doesn't really deliver gifts through a chimney has already been processed intellectually by most tweens. But as they enter the adolescent years, they will become more open to question the beliefs, values, and worldview with which they have been raised. They will begin to consider the opinions of others and become more open to different ways of looking at the world. Tweens will start to question their family's religious practices, yearly traditions, and standards of behavior. Parents need not fear this aspect of flexibility because it is a natural part of their tween's personal development.

Ideas for igniting and infusing flexibility into your tween

- As a parent (or parents), evaluate your home schedule for a typical week. What things bring structure to your tween's schedule? Sleeping in on Saturday morning, regular meals together, Friday popcorn and movie night, a time to clean their room or do laundry or take out the trash, etc.?

- Be available to listen and talk to your tween about any changes that have created anxiety in their lives at school, at home or in the world.

- Write down any significant changes or transitions you see coming in your family life that will affect your tween. Schedule a time to talk with your tween about these changes. Some changes are unavoidable, but by starting the conversation, you can help them navigate through the changes.

- As a parent (or parents), evaluate or discuss how flexible your tween really is. Brainstorm some creative ways to celebrate this value in their life.

Insights

- Flexibility means I will adapt to change.

- The wisdom of the tribe is most valuable in helping tweens adjust their dreams without destroying their passion. Flexibility opens our minds to adapting to new realities without compromising our integrity. Change comes to everyone, but those with a mindset of flexibility will navigate through life more successfully.

- Tweens will start to question their family's religious practices, yearly traditions, and standards of behavior. Parents need not fear this aspect of flexibility because it is a natural part of their tween's personal development.

CHAPTER 13

AUTHENTICITY

*"To be yourself in a world that is constantly
trying to make you something else is
the greatest accomplishment."*
– Ralph Waldo Emerson

*"The thing that is really hard, and really amazing,
is giving up on being perfect and beginning
the work of becoming yourself."*
– Anna Quindlen

Authenticity: I will be the best version of my true self.

Valuable

The virtuous value of authenticity is another significant
indicator of maturity in the life of a tween. Authenticity
reminds us that we are all unique and valuable. Every child
is unique in their fingerprints and DNA, their personalities
and aptitudes, but they are also valuable—and their value
is not based on the valuables they possess or on someone

THE THIRTEENITIES

simply saying they are of value to them. I believe every person carries within them an inherent value. They have value simply because they exist. Just like a $100 bill is always worth $100 even if it is neglected, abused, or damaged, its value does not change.

Because we are all inherently unique and valuable, we are all worthy of human dignity and respect. Each of us can enhance the human experience, just by being who we are. However, even though we are unique and valuable, each of us is imperfect, and striving to better ourselves is a worthy endeavor. We were born an original, but as we grow into maturity and authenticity, we have the opportunity to become the very best version of ourselves. Tweens are great, but they have the potential to become amazing; as parents, we get to see that happen.

ID

I do not like the term "identity theft." I don't like the crime itself, but I also am not a big fan of the name of the crime because I do not believe anyone can actually steal your identity. They can falsify, counterfeit, or copy your identification. They can even impersonate you; but no one can steal your identity. Your identity is the sum of everything that makes you, you. It's your body, your mind, your spirit, your dreams, your hurts, your frustrations, and your passions. In short, it's you. In addition to your identity, you also have cards and numbers that identify you, confirming your name, your address, or your nationality. These pieces of identification could include a passport, driver's license, or library card. These cards or numbers in a database allow you certain privileges or rights. You also have an image. An image is a representation of who you are, which may or may not be entirely accurate. Image is what others perceive you to be and can be influenced by such things as your clothing choices or social media posts. Your identification and your image can help you as you journey through life, but they are not your identity. Your identity is who you really are.

My message to parents is this: understand your tween's identification and image, but celebrate their identity and seek to inspire them to become the best that they can be. Their identification pieces and their image will change many times over their life. Infinitely more important than those, is their authentic identity.

Swords

Authenticity calls us to be ourselves, and to be the best we can be. In his legendary series *The Lord of the Rings*, J. R. R. Tolkien introduces us to the character Aragorn, who is initially revealed as Strider, a Ranger of the North. In that original courageous role he wielded the Aragorn Ranger sword and aided The Fellowship in the quest to destroy the infamous ring. In *The Return of the King*, Aragorn eventually rises up to become who he was meant to be—the rightful king of the united kingdoms of Arnor and Gondor. From that point he takes the re-forged sword named Andúril, or the Flame of the West.

I think that Sword of Strider and the Sword of the King are great images for tweens. They teach that sometimes our lives can be lived honorably serving as a ranger, but if our purpose is to be king, then we need to take up a new sword and courageously become who we were meant to be. Now, I understand this image is of weaponry and written with a male character, so I hope the message is not lost. Aragorn could have just been a co-leader of the nine in The Fellowship, and that would have been good. But he accepted the affirmation of his tribe and stepped up to become the leader of multitudes, and that was extraordinary.

Authenticity calls us to greatness, not mediocrity. Chris Hogan once said, "Somebody somewhere is in need of you becoming what you were destined to be. The only question is if you will do your part." Parents, and the tribe, can support tweens in understanding who they are and who they are meant to be.

Remember

Authenticity calls us not only to greatness, but also to goodness. My grade six teacher, Mr. Fielding, was influential in nudging me in that direction. He taught his students in many different ways to respect ourselves and respect others. I especially remember one incident.

There was a girl in my class who accidently spilled a jar of paint all over her portrait in art class. I and several others, being immature eleven-year-olds, couldn't help but giggle at her misfortune. Mr. Fielding took us aside quietly and reminded us all that was not who we really were. We weren't those who laughed at the expense of others, and that's what I remember because I agreed with Mr. Fielding—that was NOT the kind of person I was or wanted to be. He just reminded me of that important reality, and he helped me clarify my identity. I am glad for the thousands of Mr. Fieldings in the world who believe in young people.

It is important in life to find something to believe in, but it is also important to find people who believe in you. Parents can ignite and infuse authenticity into the lives of their tweens not with judgment or punishment, but by reminding them of who they really are.

Challenge

In the book *The Essential Bennis*, author Warren Bennis writes:

> "To be authentic is literally to be your own author (the words derive from the same Greek root), to discover your native energies and desires, and then find your own way of acting on them. When you have done that, you are not existing simply to live up to an image posited by the culture or by family tradition or some other authority. When you write your own life, you have played the game that was natural for you to play."

Tweens face a struggle of opposites. They want to be their own person, but they also want to fit in and be accepted as part of a group. In other words, they want to be different, just like everyone else. It is a real challenge for them because they are often more concerned with what others may think about them. Then there are some tweens that are so shy and introverted that they really don't want to be part of any group at all.

Parents, this is a real challenge for you because you want your tween to begin to understand their identity, which may cause them to stand out, but you also want them to feel socially accepted and fit in. The keys for parents are to listen carefully to their tweens, affirm their uniqueness, encourage social connection without pushing them into it, and remind them in appropriate ways of their value and worth as individuals.

As someone once said, "Always be who you are, and say what you feel, because people who mind don't matter, and people who matter don't mind."

Ideas for igniting and infusing authenticity into your tween

- Help your tween discover their fashion style and remind them that clothing often creates an image, and that their identity is far more important than their image.

- Share with another parent of a tweenager the FACTS about each of your children using the following:

  Family – their full name and why it was chosen, their birth order and siblings, their age and birthday, what family traits they have

  Attitude – what they think about school, the future, and toward life in general

  Competencies – what they like to do, what they excel at—sports, music, hobbies, academics

  Temperament – whether they are more of an introvert or extrovert, leader or follower, focused more on tasks or people, artsy or analytical

  Social life – who their friends are, and what groups, teams, clubs they connect with

- Plant a tree with your young tween child and take a photo with them beside the tree every year to see how they have both continued to grow and mature into who they are becoming.

Insights

- Authenticity means I will be the best version of my true self.

- Authenticity reminds us that we are all unique and valuable. We were born an original, but as we grow into maturity and authenticity, we have the opportunity to become the very best version of ourselves. Tweens are great, but they have the potential to become amazing; as parents, we get to see that happen.

- Understand your tween's identification and image, but celebrate their identity and seek to inspire them to become the best that they can be. Their identification pieces and their image will change many times over their life. Infinitely more important than those, is their authentic identity.

CHAPTER 14

SPIRITUALITY

"Sometimes people get the mistaken notion that spirituality is a separate department of life, the penthouse of existence. But rightly understood, it is a vital awareness that pervades all realms of our being."

— David Steindl-Rast

"No matter how much we try to run away from this thirst for the answer to life, for the meaning of life, the intensity only gets stronger and stronger. We cannot escape these spiritual hungers."

— Ravi Zacharias

Spirituality: I will seek to discover the meaning of life.

Quest

Of all the Thirteenities, spirituality is the most difficult to define. It carries with it the idea of meaning and purpose, worship and reverence, deeper and grander experiences, tradition and practice, belief and faith. The mantra of many North Americans today is that they are "spiritual but not religious." To me, that is just like saying, "I'm romantic, just not currently dating anyone." I think that religion is just spirituality that has aligned itself with one particular set of beliefs and practices, just like dating or marriage is romance that has simply aligned itself with just one other person.

One image that has described spirituality or religion over the centuries is that of a quest, which is a search for something. It usually is a search for that which is currently unknown, unlike a quest to find a missing sock from the laundry. The only thing unknown about the sock is its location. A spiritual quest has questions. Although very few people leave their job or drop out of school to embark on this quest, I have found many people think about these questions in the everyday flow of their lives. Who am I? Why am I here? What is the meaning or purpose of my life? Is there a God? If there is a God, what does God want from me, if anything?

Tweens will begin to ask these questions as well. Because their thinking is moving from the concrete to the abstract, they can start to consider these questions and take the first steps on their spiritual quest. Parents will need to be aware that spiritual questions and discussions will come your way, so it is helpful to be prepared.

Faith

In the New Testament of the Christian Bible, in the book of James 2:26, it says, "As the body without the spirit is dead, so faith without deeds is dead." This means that spiritual belief and intellectual theology without some kind of activity that flows from it is like a body void of life. The structure exists, but it is dead. Throughout history, both wonderful and horrific acts have been done in the name of religion, just as there have been wonderful and horrific acts done by those with no religious motivation.

I am most impressed by the positive change that has been brought on by individuals who came from a spiritual or religious heritage like Mohandas Karamchand Gandhi (Hindu), Mother Teresa (Roman Catholic), Dr. Martin Luther King Jr. (Baptist), and Nelson Mandela (Methodist). What is most interesting about these and others who have brought significant social change is that it seemed like their actions, even though motivated by their faith, were not necessarily done to bring others into it. Their actions were simply to serve humanity and to try to make right, things that were unjust, like poverty and human inequality. Their stories are extraordinary, although they themselves are quite ordinary people. It was their sacrificial and loving actions that made the difference.

Tweens are also people of action. They have an inclination toward compassion and justice. And as they begin to explore spirituality, they will be most influenced by those who do as well—people with faith and good deeds.

Heaven

One of the big questions people on a spiritual quest have is, "What happens after we die?" There has been much speculation, teaching, imagination, and discussion about this. Being a funeral celebrant, I am well aware of this question because everyone at a funeral understands that it's just Aunt Ruth's bodily remains in the casket or urn; it's not really her. Her life has left her body. The question is, "Where is Aunt Ruth? If there really is a heaven, is she there?" I won't and honestly can't answer that question based upon any hard facts and conclusive evidence, but here's what I do know. If there is a heaven, one first-century Middle Eastern rabbi taught his followers to pray, "Thy kingdom come, Thy will be done, on Earth as it is in heaven." Was he suggesting that heaven could be brought to Earth? I think so, and here's how I saw it happen.

Many years ago I accepted a part-time position as a support worker for a social service agency in my hometown. My job was to seek out volunteer activities for a twenty-something man with Down syndrome. I'll call him Anthony. Anthony and I would spend every Friday morning together cleaning an auto shop waiting room, raking leaves, or shoveling snow. Anthony was amazing, and Friday mornings were the highlight of my week!

Every year, all the support workers were invited with their friends to attend an Oktoberfest celebration at a local dance hall. The room would be filled with over 100 special needs and handicapped children and adults, many of whom had severe disabilities and had been in wheelchairs since birth. Each of these individuals had their own personal support worker who graciously accommodated this event. Oktoberfest sausage on a bun was served, and of course, some of those who needed assistance eating had their food liquefied in a blender so that they could drink it through a straw because it was the only way they could ingest it. There were balloons and decorations and a spirited oompa band playing festive music that filled the hall. It was so loud that some had to cover their ears. The room echoed with the grunts of some of these beautiful individuals who were unable to speak, but who were obviously caught up in the excitement of the moment. The highlight for me was when the band announced they were going to play the "Chicken Dance" song, an obvious favorite. Cheers erupted and the guests were wheeled out to the dance floor.

And then it happened. Without warning or preparation, I saw a glimpse of heaven. It wasn't in a cathedral or at a remote waterfall in some tropical forest. It wasn't in the singing of a great hymn or in seeing a magnificent piece of art. It was in an Oktoberfest beerhall, smelling of sweat and blended sausages and buns, where 100 severely disabled people, strapped to their wheelchairs and aided by their dedicated support workers, with pure and childlike joy and celebration, danced the "Chicken Dance"! It was all transcendent—the unbridled outburst of ecstasy, the sacrifice and love of those there to help and serve, the music, and most of all, the look of absolute happiness on the faces of my wheelchair dancing friends. It was truly heaven on Earth.

In their search for the spiritual, tweens may encounter something like I did one Friday morning in October. They may not find the complete answer to their questions, but they will discover just enough to motivate them to stay on the journey. They may never connect to a church, a synagogue, a mosque, or a temple, but they will continue on their quest. Parents should encourage such a quest, in spite of the failings of religion and the evil things done in its name. The world will be a better place when the tweens grow up and fill the gaps left by Gandhi, Mother Teresa, Nelson Mandela, and Martin Luther King Jr.

Ideas for igniting and infusing spirituality into your tween

- Discuss with your tween your personal spiritual quest. For some that will include identifying with a particular religious group. Affirm the good things about your faith tradition, and be honest and acknowledge its errors and shortcomings of the group in the past.

- Attend a religious service with your tween, especially if that is not your normal practice. This will help them better understand a specific religious denomination or group.

- Purchase religious texts to have in your home to be more personally aware of what they actually say.

- Check out any spiritual youth groups your tween could be involved in. Many will include a social and recreational aspect to their programming.

Insights

- Spirituality means I will seek to discover the meaning of life.

- Of all the Thirteenities, spirituality is the most difficult to define. I think that religion is just spirituality that has aligned itself with one particular set of beliefs and practices, just like dating or marriage is romance that has simply aligned itself with just one other person.

- Tweens are also people of action. They have an inclination toward compassion and justice. And as they begin to explore spirituality, they will be most influenced by those who do as well—people with faith and good deeds. They may never connect to a church, a synagogue, a mosque, or a temple, but they will continue on their quest. Parents should encourage such a quest, in spite of the failings of religion and the evil things done in its name.

CHAPTER 15

CURIOSITY

*"Somewhere, something incredible
is waiting to be known."*

– Carl Sagan

*"The barrier during self-improvement is not so
much that we hate learning, rather we hate being
taught. To learn entails that the knowledge was
achieved on one's own accord - it feels great - but
to be taught often leaves a feeling of inferiority.
Thus it takes a bit of determination and a lot of
humility in order for one to fully develop."*

– Criss Jami

Curiosity: I will continue to learn.

School

For thirty-five years my father was an elementary school
teacher and vice principal. Because he was transferred to
many schools, my dad was well known, and by association

because of our shared unique last name, so was I. Being a typical second-born child, and growing up in the shadow of my typical type-A personality older brother, I had the cards stacked against me when I started to attend school.

I was known as Roy's boy (my dad's name was obviously Roy), or as Paul's brother (I was two years younger). My dad was an educator, my brother was an honor-roll student who went on to become a successful chemical engineer, and I had a first name that rhymed with several bad words, so as you can imagine, I hated school. I didn't hate everything about it, just the classroom, homework, and learning parts; everything else was fine. I was not a good student and had trouble concentrating in class. My marks hovered around the 60 percent neighborhood, which allowed me to pass every year, but just barely. The profound irony in all of this is that I eventually went on to get a degree in education and spent fourteen years as a part-time adjunct professor at two local colleges. Life is indeed funny.

The point here is that I am a strong believer in education, some of which can actually happen at school. You will not find me improperly criticizing teachers; I have great respect for them and the role they play in the lives of tweens. But sometimes the system in which they find themselves makes it difficult for students to learn. Schools are often underfunded, understaffed, and weighed down with red tape. Parents need to take the leadership in understanding how their tween learns and seek to provide the best opportunity they can, given the resources they have. What every parent can do is seek to instill a natural curiosity in their children, so learning and growth become accepted and expected. The value of curiosity has been embraced by great women and men throughout history. These are the ones who were the inventers, explorers, and often the rebels of their time. Parents can champion that value in their tweens as well.

Risk

Curiosity will take us out of our comfort zones, and learning will cause us to change. Just like fear is a threat to flexibility, boredom is a threat to curiosity. Flexibility is the value needed to react or respond to things outside our control that have changed. Curiosity is the value needed to inspire learning that will result in change inside us. Curiosity requires some risk. We need to be willing to intentionally venture into what is unknown in order for it to become known. That risk could be fairly insignificant, like reading a book, attending a class or seminar, doing research online, or having a conversation with someone who understands the subject matter.

The greater risks often come with the application of the knowledge. In other words, you can read a book about swimming, talk to people who swim, attend a class on how to swim, and do a Google search on swimming to research the topic yourself. You can know everything there is to know about swimming without ever getting into the water. The risk might seem too great for you.

A tween's learning and personal development can be hindered because they are unwilling to take a risk and venture into new waters. A supportive and affirming parent or gatekeeper can nudge a tween to take a reasonable, calculated risk.

Mountain

I have always been afraid of heights. Several years ago, at a leadership event in British Columbia, I made some progress in conquering that fear. The class activity for one of the days was to rappel down the side of a mountain. This was a huge risk for me, but I was very curious about how it would feel being suspended by a rope on the side of a rock face. I also wanted to know if I had the guts to actually do it. The instructors walked us through the entire process, often explaining that the ropes would hold, that this was a safe activity, and so on. It was a chilly day, but my hands were sweating through the entire instruction time.

Finally, it came time to start, and I watched as several of my colleagues actually rappelled down the eighty-foot cliff and arrived safely at the bottom. In fact, I watched all of them do it until finally there was just me and one other student named Kari left at the top with the instructors. I am large man, but Kari was larger. He was a professional football player, and like me, he was afraid of heights. So we agreed to rappel down at the same time. We got harnessed in, had a quick review of what was going to happen, and backed our way to the edge of the cliff. The instructor repeated over and over again, "Trust the rope. Just trust the rope, and you will be OK." There is a moment in rappelling where you lean back over the edge and your total weight is being supported by the rope. Kari and I collectively weighed well over a quarter of a ton; I thought, even if the ropes hold, the mountain might fall over. But we did it, together. We took a calculated risk, and we now know what it is like to rappel down a rock face in British Columbia.

The risks we took were not irresponsible; the instructors were certified and experienced. The experience was done with a group of supportive peers, and every precaution was taken to ensure our safety. I could have just watched everyone else go down the cliff and not gone myself. But frankly, my curiosity got the best of me, and I do not regret it.

Parents can encourage their tweens to take calculated risks when it comes to learning and personal development. They can celebrate with their tweens when they take a risk, remembering never to embarrass them if they are not ready to do so. We all have different levels of comfort when it comes to taking risks.

Story

Curiosity, which leads to a journey of learning and self-improvement, will also leave us with stories to tell. Like the quest imagery we discussed in the chapter on spirituality, curiosity will lead us on a path with many questions. A commitment to go on a journey of lifelong learning will result in many stories to tell. Much of this book has included my story. I certainly do not think my life is any better than the next person's, but it's my story and I have the scars as well as the laugh lines to prove it.

I am often saddened to hear how easily some people give up on learning, especially with the multitude of resources and opportunities we are afforded today. The childlike wonder and curiosity about the world somehow get drained out of their lives. They plateau and stop growing. I once heard someone say, "If you stop learning today, you will stop growing tomorrow."

Tweens should be encouraged not only to "question everything," but to stay curious and confident enough to ask good questions. There is a difference. They learn to respectfully discuss and debate things that they have always thought to be true with those who have a different perspective. And they should collect stories of their quest along the way. The willingness to go on a journey gives you the content for a good story.

Albert Einstein once said, "Do not grow old, no matter how long you live. Never cease to stand like curious children before the Great Mystery into which we were born." And he seemed like a pretty smart guy.

Ideas for igniting and infusing curiosity into your tween

- Take a trip with your tween that includes a learning element about another culture or historical event.

- Don't ask your tween how their day was or how school was. Ask specific questions about the subjects they are taking, ask about who they spoke to, ask about what they found frustrating. Take an interest in their education and, more than that, what interests them.

- Don't overload your tween with extracurricular activities, but do encourage them to try something totally new to see if they might like it. Community centers often offer a wide variety of programs.

- Give books as gifts for birthdays and other special occasions and help to create a love for reading in the lives of your children.

Insights

- Curiosity means I will continue to learn.

- The value of curiosity has been embraced by great women and men throughout history. These are the ones who were the inventers, explorers, and often the rebels of their time. Curiosity will take us out of our comfort zones, and learning will cause us to change

- A tween's learning and personal development can be hindered because they are unwilling to take a risk and venture into new waters. Parents can nudge a tween to take a reasonable, calculated risk. They can celebrate with their tweens when they take a risk, remembering never to embarrass them if they are not ready to do so. We all have different levels of comfort when it comes to taking risks.

CHAPTER 16

CREATIVITY

"Go into the arts. I'm not kidding. The arts are not a way to make a living. They are a very human way of making life more bearable. Practicing an art, no matter how well or badly, is a way to make your soul grow, for heaven's sake. Sing in the shower. Dance to the radio. Tell stories. Write a poem to a friend, even a lousy poem. Do it as well as you possibly can. You will get an enormous reward. You will have created something."

– Kurt Vonnegut

"The creative adult is the child who has survived."
– Ursula K. Le Guin

Creativity: I will express myself.

Birth

The final of the Thirteenities, and one of the most fun, is the value of creativity. This virtuous value is a sibling to spirituality and curiosity. Through this book we have seen how the principal value of maturity is expressed through responsibility, integrity, and authenticity and that each of those is revealed in three other virtues. It's like grandmother Maturity had three daughters and each of them had three daughters as well. They are all members of the same family, and like many families, they are inseparably intertwined. Creativity is like the wild child. She is messy and smart, sometimes absent-minded, but incredibly deep and insightful. She dresses differently than her siblings and cousins, she has a bit of a harsh tongue at times, but she is beautiful beyond measure.

I believe every person carries within them this measure of beauty and creativity. In the first verse of the Hebrew Scriptures, we read, "In the beginning, God created..." In the narrative of that faith tradition, humans were made in the image of God and were imprinted with the amazing attribute of creativity. Maybe that's why you occasionally hear thanks given to God during an acceptance speech at the Emmys or Grammys. These artists may be acknowledging in some way that, even though they worked hard in refining their craft, the actual creative ability was granted to them at birth. Or maybe not. Either way, it seems to be true that everyone has some creativity when they are born.

Every child may be born an artist, but unfortunately they lose that passion as they leave their childhood behind. The problem is how to remain an artist once he grows up. Parents can help their tweens continue on the path of creative understanding and expression. When children are young, their artwork gets proudly displayed on the refrigerator. There is a time that stops happening, and I am sure there are many reasons for that, but one of those reasons should never be that a parent wants to obstruct their child's creative expression.

Art

We often think of creativity as it relates to the arts, including music, dance, and the fine arts. Creativity goes much deeper than that. She crosses into business, where product and service innovation are critical. Creativity is necessary in architecture, advertising, entertainment, technology, education, health care, and almost every other sector—except accounting; creative bookkeeping has a poor reputation. However, creative problem solving is a vital asset to any organization. Creative communication, creative solutions, and creative advancements are all good things. So just because a person does not break-dance or finger paint, that does not exclude them from using their creative energies in the space in which they find themselves.

Parents can encourage their tweens to be creative in solving everyday problems, or to use their imagination to envision a future where they could find happiness and meaning. They can also celebrate their tween's interest in break-dance finger painting.

Hair

Tweens will find a way to express themselves, often with no encouragement from an outside source. They may start to wear a different style of clothing, change their hairstyle or color, or even redecorate their bedroom. They may wish to do one or more of these to fit in with their friends, to genuinely express themselves, or just to get a reaction from their parents. These are all normal desires, and the best advice for parents is to not overreact.

The key is to connect with your tween as best as you can, to spend time listening to them, and to seek to understand their motive for choosing why they want to express themselves in such a way. This is where a discerning mind is so important.

Parents will want to selectively choose what expressions are worth arguing over and which ones are not worth the energy to battle. Most times tweens will grow out of that particular creative expression, just like their parents did when they were a tween. How many of us have the same hairstyle we had when we were in grade six? So the balance here is to encourage creative expression for your tween, but also to expect that the specific creative expressions they choose might be a shock to you.

Curiosity is a lifelong commitment to take in learning and new experiences, while creativity is the lifelong invitation to express learning, experiences, and life as we understand it.

Ideas for igniting and infusing creativity into your tween

- Talk to your tween about what areas of artistic expression are of interest to them, then assist them in pursuing it. That might include paying for guitar lessons, dance classes, or a pottery course.

- Keep some of the artwork your tween creates in a keepsake box as a way to celebrate their creative aptitude.

- Go to places with your tween (and their friends) that celebrate the arts—a music festival, art gallery, or museum.

- Agree as parents that you will not freak out when your tween reveals a major change in their hairstyle, clothing choice, or room décor. Also agree that listening and connecting with them at such a time will be your top priority.

Insights

- Creativity means I will express myself.

- This virtuous value is a sibling to spirituality and curiosity.

- Creativity crosses into business, where product and service innovation are critical. Creativity is necessary in architecture, advertising, entertainment, technology, education, health care, and almost every other sector.

- Curiosity is a lifelong commitment to take in learning and new experiences, while creativity is the lifelong invitation to express learning, experiences, and life as we understand it.

CHAPTER 17

THE COMING OF AGE CEREMONY

"What you leave behind is not what is engraved in stone monuments, but what is woven into the lives of others."
— Pericles

*"Parents rarely let go of their children,
so children let go of them.
They move on. They move away.
The moments that used to define them - a mother's
approval, a father's nod - are covered by moments of
their own accomplishments. It is not until much later,
as the skin sags and the heart weakens, that children
understand; their stories, and all their accomplishments,
sit atop the stories of their mothers and fathers, stones
upon stones, beneath the waters of their lives."*
— Mitch Albom

Almost every culture in the world has a common event that marks and celebrates when an individual passes from childhood into adulthood—but not in North America. There are several events we unofficially identify in this category: turning thirteen or sixteen, getting your driver's license, losing your virginity, entering or graduating from high school, or becoming eligible to vote. But we have no common event to mark this occasion.

Throughout history, the "coming-of-age" ceremony or rite of passage was known as a gathering where the leaders and other members of the tribe publically affirm that a child is ready to be welcomed into adulthood. The age when this happens differs depending on the culture and community, but it is normally from age twelve to sixteen. The purpose of this event is not to burden a child with undue expectations or responsibilities they would be unable to fulfill—on the contrary. It is actually a moment that identifies and celebrates the reality that every tween will cross the bridge from childhood into adulthood. It acknowledges that every other human being has had to experience that transition and that the tween will be supported by the tribe through this part of their life journey. It is indeed a celebration.

Such ceremonies often include some of the following elements:

- Invitations to family members, friends of the family, peers of the child, and community or spiritual leaders to participate in the event

- A test the child must pass to prove she is ready to be counted among the adult members of the tribe

- Words of encouragement and charge to the child from a leader of their community

- Presentation of a gift of significance to the child that represents the responsibilities of an adult member of the tribe

- Corporate expressions of worship or gratitude to a deity for the life of the child as they move into adulthood

- Words of blessing and affirmation spoken to the child by their parents or other significant adults

- The reading of a creed or manifesto that identifies what it means to be an adult member of the tribe

- Sharing of a meal

- Enjoying music and dancing

- Wearing special clothing that mark the celebration

For members of a spiritual community, these celebrations are a regular part of their faith tradition and practice. Some examples would be the Rite of Confirmation practiced by Roman Catholic Church or the Jewish Bar Mitzvah or Bat Mitzvah ceremonies. However, with the significantly decreased involvement in faith communities in North America and the increase in the number of broken and blended families, I believe an opportunity is missing for parents and their tweens.

I believe that every tween can and should have a ceremony that welcomes them into adulthood. Further, I believe that tweens actually desire this and that we have let them down in not doing so. We have unintentionally and unknowingly given them permission to extend their emotional and social adolescence well into their adult years. Our children have grown older chronologically, without having grown up. This extended adolescent mindset has halted their desire to move into the world and create their own life. Inspiring and igniting into our tweens the value of maturity and the other Thirteenities and celebrating their entrance into this next stage of life is a gift parents must give their children. It is truly a gift beyond measure. I sincerely invite all parents to consider this as a significant event in the life of their tween and their tribe.

A coming-of-age celebration could be part of a thirteenth birthday party for your child or held at another regular family gathering. Parents would want to begin considering this early, perhaps when your child is eleven or twelve years old. You will need to discuss this with your tween and clearly communicate the purpose of such an event—when and where it could be held and what it would look like. Because of the nature of this event, I would also confirm that your tween is open to this, and that it not be forced upon them. It may not resonate with some tweens, and might be better left to a much later time or not take place at all.

If your tween is open to such an event, you would begin to plan it together. Make sure the event is filled with a variety of fun, age-appropriate activities. Parents could work with their tween to decide who would participate and what they would like to have included. Tweens that are more introverted or shy would not want to be the center of attention, so the focus might be on having a smaller, more intimate gathering of the tribe. Here are some things that could be included in a coming-of-age ceremony.

- A guest list created by the tween and parents that would include immediate and extended family members, friends of the tween, friends of the parents, mentors, teachers, coaches, significant adults in the life of the tween, and even religious, spiritual, or community leaders

- Fun activities that both tweens and adults could participate in together like sports, camping, an overnight trip, a ropes course, or hiking

- An emcee for the gathering time

- A list of those who might share some words of affirmation (e.g., words from peers of the tween, a mentor, a family member, or a spiritual or community leader)

- Presentation of a gift of significance to the tween, which can be kept secret from the child until the ceremony itself, and which could be a family heirloom, a gift that carries an obvious connection to a character quality like a piece of art or other decorative piece, or even a financial gift in the form of a savings bond

- The reading of a manifesto, creed, or other special reading that helps to communicate what adulthood means to the family (e.g., "The Road Not Taken" by Robert Frost or "If: A Father's Advice to His Son" by Rudyard Kipling)

- For spiritual families, there might be a reading, blessing, or prayer from a sacred text or even a spiritual but nondenominational book, like an ancient Franciscan blessing

- Appetizers or a full meal

- Music, either live or recorded, and dancing

- Buying your tween some new clothes to wear for the celebration

- A guestbook to record all who attended or other keepsake with a way for them to express their congratulations to the tween

- For further ideas and resources, check out www.thethirteenities.com

The key for parents is to do something for their tweens that affirms them and welcomes them into adulthood—big or small, extravagant or simple. Even a note written to a tween by one or both parents can be a treasured keepsake reminding the child of the adventure and often adversity of adult life.

Insights

- Almost every culture in the world has a common event that marks and celebrates when an individual passes from childhood into adulthood—but not in North America.

- Throughout history, the "coming-of-age" ceremony or rite of passage was known as a gathering where the leaders and other members of the tribe publically affirm that a child is ready to be welcomed into adulthood.

- A coming-of-age celebration could be part of a thirteenth birthday party for your child or held at another regular family gathering. The key for parents is to do something for their tweens that affirms them and welcomes them into adulthood—big or small, extravagant or simple.

CHAPTER 18

FINALLY

"Unconditional love is love without requiring anything in return - love no matter what. Love never fails."

– Heather Forbes

"And now these three remain: faith, hope and love. But the greatest of these is love."

– Saint Paul

Love

The ethic of love is woven into all the religious traditions of the world: love for God, for self, for others, for nature, and for the universe. It is also embraced by those who do not identify with any particular religious tradition. In my mind it is the greatest of all the great virtuous values. It is the highest human virtue and often the most needed. I did not include it in the thirteen virtuous values because it deserves its own, unique place.

Not to put too fine a point on this thought, but parents, your child is a product of your love. A loving environment and love communicated in appropriate ways will create the framework for the Thirteenities to be expressed to your tween. It takes a loving parent and loving members of the tribe to better enable a tween to face the realities of growing up. A parent cannot control many things for their tween, but one thing they can control is their commitment to love their child unconditionally. I see that love demonstrated every week when I speak with parents and see how they interact with their children.

So, if after having read this book, you are not convinced that it is a worthy investment to seek to ignite and infuse these thirteen virtuous values into the life of your tween, my most sincere hope is that you will always commit to loving your child unconditionally.

Grace

There is much pressure placed on parents today. Societal expectations are very high. The margin for error seems slim. Raising children in a culture that has a plurality of moral values, an inundation of information, and an accelerated rate of change has created more confusion than clarity for parents. The good news is this: parenting is sometimes overrated. I don't mean parents shouldn't do all they can to be good parents. Obviously every parent should aim to be as good as they can be. But the reality is that even children who have had "bad parents" (whatever that means) often turn out to be successful in life.

That is not to say there won't be emotional scars or bad memories. I think most adults have those. I know I do. But, it is in those very memories that forgiveness and reconciliation can be experienced. The hurtful past can be an excuse for us to choose resentment, or it can be the foundation of a life of extraordinary grace. In a world of imperfect parents and imperfect children, I recommend living by grace, rooted in love, filled with hope.

Symphony

Mr. Holland's Opus is a movie about a reluctant music teacher. Mr. Holland did not want to teach high school students, but for thirty years he did, and he came to love the students. In the end, his job was cut because of budget constraints. He felt as if he had given it all for nothing. Nobody cared. Nobody would even remember. It was all over. As he walked down the long empty school hall for the last time with his son and wife at his side, he heard noise coming from the auditorium. He opened the door and found it full of his former students. They had come to say thanks.

One little girl whom he had taught the clarinet was now the state governor. She walked to the podium and said:

> "Rumor had it that Mr. Holland was always working on this symphony of his. And this was going to make him famous, rich, probably both. But Mr. Holland isn't rich, and he isn't famous at least not outside of our little town. So it might be easy for him to think himself a failure. And he would be wrong, because I think he's achieved a success far beyond riches and fame. Look around you. There is not a life in this room that you have not touched. And each one of us is a better person because of you. We are your symphony, Mr. Holland. We are the melodies and the notes of your opus. And we are the music of your life."

Parents, the investments you make in the lives of your children are the most significant accomplishments you will leave behind on this Earth. Parenting is difficult, but always worth it. Celebrate that today. My hope for you and for every parent is that you will find incredible joy in your children. I wish you extraordinary success as parents.

"Few will have the greatness to bend history itself, but each of us can work to change a small portion of events, and in the total of all those acts will be written the history of this generation."

– Robert F. Kennedy

Insights

- The ethic of love is woven into all the religious traditions of the world and it is also embraced by those who do not identify with any particular religious tradition. In my mind it is the greatest of all the great virtuous values I did not include it in the thirteen virtuous values because it deserves its own, unique place. A loving environment and love communicated in appropriate ways will create the framework for the Thirteenities to be expressed to your tween

- There is much pressure placed on parents today. Societal expectations are very high. It is in the emotional scars and very memories that forgiveness and reconciliation can be experienced.

- The investments parents make in the lives of your children are the most significant accomplishments they will leave behind on this Earth. Parenting is difficult, but always worth it.

About the Author

Martti Pajunen is a Canadian writer, inspirational speaker, transformational coach, and Life Celebration Specialist. His Finnish heritage comes through his grandparents who immigrated to Canada in the 1930's. Born and raised in Kitchener Ontario, the second oldest of 4 boys and the son of a Sr. Elementary school teacher, Martti grew up playing hockey, loving the outdoors, and appreciating the value of learning life lessons through his family, school, and youth group.

Martti grew up in a conservative church tradition and after graduating from college, served within the denomination for 25 years as Minister to Students and Families, consultant, college professor, and denominational youth director to 300 churches in Ontario and Quebec.

He has worked as an event planner with numerous professional sports teams in creating and running big events for students.

As a Licensed Wedding Officiant and Certified Funeral Celebrant, Martti has conducted over 1700 weddings ceremonies and 700 funeral services, serving people from all walks of life.

Exercising his creative and entrepreneurial thinking, Martti has launched several unique initiatives and businesses, aligning himself with like-minded agencies and individuals to achieve win-win-win successes. He is the lead facilitator of the "From the Ground Up", a corporate team-building exercise program at Strom's Farm in Guelph, Ontario. He has mentored dozens of couples as a Certified Relationship Coach. He recently entered the fashion industry when he launched marties, a division of the Olive and Arthur Clothing Company in Cambridge, Ontario. The name marties plays on

THE THIRTEENITIES

a nickname he had as a child because of the unique spelling of his Scandinavian name. Turning a negative into a sustainable positive, marties produces sophisticated wedding bow tie sets from recycled, and sometimes memory, fabric.

Martti has passionately influenced adolescents to live lives of greatness and goodness in a variety of leadership roles.

The book, *The Thirteenities: leading tweens to loves of greatness and goodness*, has been a long time initiative that has evolved over the years to what it is today. It is now the foundational piece of a movement that is seeking to transform how parents view their role, especially in dealing with their children during the tween years, from ages 9 to 12.

The quick fix, behavioural modification model of punishment and reward has been the standard of parenting for decades in North America. The role of parent has often been demoted from benevolent leader to simply an adult friend. The numerous agencies that were supporting the infusion of universally accepted virtues and values into the lives of children have been replaced with a tsunami of mixed media messages, leaving many parents feeling lost, irrelevant and fearful. *The Thirteenities* are defined as a collection of thirteen virtuous values that parents can ignite and infuse in the lives of tweens leading them toward lives of greatness and goodness. It is a refreshing approach to parenting that begins with fresh mindset to see parenting as leadership and the modelling of virtuous values as the primary goal. This approach is less of a roadmap and more of a compass. In the book and accompanying on-line training, Martti affirms and inspires parents in their role. His warmth in communicating and humorous stories invites parents to not only investigate, but to actually commit to leading their children to lives of greatness and goodness. Martti enjoys hockey, motorcycling, stand-up comedy, and attending the occasional blues festival. Find out more about Martti and the book at www.thethirteenities.com

About Martti's Business

Ever since I was a teenager, I have found great success and joy by inspiring early adolescents to live lives of greatness and goodness. That passion has continued into my adult years as I have held numerous positions from volunteer youth drug addiction mentor, to college professor, and international keynote speaker.

Through hundreds of conversations with parents and teenagers and years of studying pre-adolescent and youth culture and behavior, my conclusions led me to write the book *The Thirteenities [thur-TEEN-i-tees]:* leading tweens to lives of greatness and goodness.

The book is like a preseason training manual for parents of tweens (children age 9 to 12) where they are introduced to The Thirteenities, a collection of virtuous values that they can ignite and infuse in the lives of tweens leading them toward lives of greatness and goodness. The book has led to the birth of a company of the same name. My dream is to see families transformed as parents *commit to live these values and lead their children to do so as well.*

My company provides electronic and hardcopy resources for parents, on-line parent training, and information about live events. I am available to provide corporate keynote speaking services, parenting seminars, and inspirational talks to student and love to partner with groups committed to leading young people toward lives of greatness and goodness.

Learn more and connect with me at:
www.thethirteenities.com

Connect with the Author

Website: www.thethirteenities.com

Email: martti@thethirteenities.com

Facebook: https://www.facebook.com/martti.pajunen

Facebook: The Thirteenities (Public Group) https://www.facebook.com/groups/263692040633461/?ref =bookmarks

LinkedIn: https://www.linkedin.com/in/martti-pajunen-965a0110

Twitter: @marttipajunen

Instagram: marttipajunen

Acknowledgements

Two of the virtuous values I identify in my book, *The Thirteenities*, are community and humility. I have experienced both of those in great measure as I have worked on this project. I have been very fortunate in my life to not only have a village, but also a tribe.

My village is comprised of every business and social relationship, from local to international that has enhanced and added value to my life and provided me the opportunity to do the same for them. My tribe, however, is made up of those who identify with me in a much deeper way relationally. I am eternally grateful for my tribe of friends and family members who have helped and supported me in the quest to complete this project. Some have walked with me for years while others joined me for a brief time. However, each one joined with me at just the right time in my journey, providing wisdom, encouragement, and companionship. I gratefully acknowledge and appreciate each of these individuals. I humbly acknowledge and express thanks for these wonderful people.

For my amazing children and source of inspiration, Mariah, Brianne, and Maxfield.

For my grandchildren, who I believe are the hope for this world, Lincoln, Everlee, Gavin, and Charleigh.

For Trish, their wonderful and loving mother and now, nana.

For my parents, Alice (deceased) and Roy, along with my brothers Paul, Steve and Tim and their families.

For my amigos who walked with me through the darkest times of my life, Tim Bailey, John Blackman, Gerry Gould, David McKenna, Norm Veevers, and my two brothers who have since left this earth, Steve Baxter and Peter McNeily.

For my publisher, Robbin Simons and her team.

For Wayne and Rosanne Prevett and the associates at Kettle Creek Weddings and Celebrating Life Ministries.

For my editing friends, Denise Bott, Kathy Hurst, Lisa Roeck, Mariah Roeck, and Wendy Saulesleja.

For my creative and technical advisors, Kevin Brandon, Lindsay Coulter, Taylor Jackson, and Timothy Muza.

For Melody Hunter who designed the book cover and Tim Bailey who designed the amazing Thirteenities logo.

For my crazy motorcycle buddies, David "Sweet D", Julie, and Tom.

For the many people I have met along the way who affirmed me and the value of this endeavor, Wendy Arthurs, Steve and Libby Blakely, Sylvie Beaucage, Kevin and Denise Bott, Trudy Bricker, Christine Cardoza, Dave Chilton, Roy Cleeves, Mike and Karen Connelly, Eric Deschamps, John and Maureen Dinner, Evan Garst, Bev Gay, Zane and Marcia Grant, Al and Irene Harder, Grace Howe, Joanne Jones, Dean Kennedy, Cindy Middleton, Kimberley "K" Murray, Sharon Parenteau, Karen Richmond, Aaron Roeck, Cheryl Schade, Martin and Sherry Slejska, Colin Sprake, Anne Warren, Brad Watson, and Mike Yaconelli.

And finally for the dozens of teachers, youth workers, professors, coaches, creative thinkers, and volunteer leaders who have influenced my life over the years. I hope you know that your efforts were not in vain.

In Appreciation

Thank you for purchasing *The Thirteenities*. My dream is that your family will be transformed by understanding these virtuous values and by committing to live them out every day. I commend you for your interest in the content of the book, and truly celebrate with those who have made a commitment to lead their children to lives of greatness and goodness. If that is your decision, I invite you to help me to serve many other families as well.

Here's how you can do that...

- Let other parents of tweens know about the book and online video training series through your social and professional networks.

- Share this resource with your school parent's committee, local volunteer organization, church group, or other organization that supports parents of tweens or adolescents.

- Invite Martti to speak at your next event – a workplace "lunch and learn", a corporate function, a parent training event through your school, church or community group.

- Write a customer review of *The Thirteenities* at www. amazon.com

References

CHAPTER 1: INTRODUCTION

Rick Pitino, who said, *"Failure is good. It's fertilizer. Everything I've learned about coaching, I have learned from making mistakes."*

http://www.successories.com/iquote/category/121/american-athlete-quotes/65

CHAPTER 2: WHAT ARE THE THIRTEENITIES?

Words

The legendary actor and comedian Robin Williams once said, *"No matter what people tell you, words and ideas can change the world."*

http://www.business.com/quotes/no-matter-what-people-tell-you-words-and-ideas-can-change-the-world/

Virtuous Values

The original Latin word virtus meant "valor" or "moral perfection."

https://en.wikipedia.org/wiki/Virtue

Parents

"gatekeepers."

https://en.wikipedia.org/wiki/Gatekeeper

Ignite and infuse

"Infuse" means to pour in, to cause to be permeated, or to introduce one thing into another so as to change it forever.

http://www.merriam-webster.com/dictionary/infuse

Tweens

The term "tween" was really first coined by J.R.R. Tolkien in his 1954 novel *The Fellowship of the Ring*.

There is some discussion about who originally coined the term that closest resembles the current meaning. The term tweenie actually shows up in Christopher Morley's Kathleen which was published in 1918. Regarding Kathleen; *"She was that most adorable of creatures, the tweenie, between girl and woman, with the magic of both and the weaknesses of neither.* (Chapter 8)

Leading them

Wikipedia says, *"Parenting or child rearing is the process of promoting and supporting the physical, emotional, social, financial, and intellectual development of a child from infancy to adulthood. Parenting refers to the aspects of raising a child aside from the biological relationship."*

https://en.wikipedia.org/wiki/Parenting

"Leadership is the capacity to translate vision into reality." (Warren Bennis)

Cited in: Dianna Daniels Booher (1991) Executive's portfolio of model speeches for all occasions.

"Leadership is influence—nothing more, nothing less." (John Maxwell)

The 21 Irrefutable Laws of Leadership: Follow Them and People Will Follow You, by John Maxwell. Revised, Updated, 10th Anniversary ed. edition (April 1, 2014). Chapter 2.

Greatness and goodness

The V-twin engine used by several motorcycle companies is made with two twin cylinders that are manufactured in the shape of a V—therefore, the name "V-twin."

For more information on the history of the Harley Davidson V Twin engine, see https://www.harley-davidson.com/content/h-d/en_US/home/museum/explore/hd-history/1900.html

CHAPTER 3: THE PRESEASON

Eric Erikson

From Erik Erikson's Childhood and Society (published in 1950) He expanded and refined his theory in later books.

Thomas Armstrong

From http://www.institute4learning.com/stages_of_life.php

Emotions

The Mighty Canadian Minebuster™ *is* one of 3 wooden roller coasters at *Paramount Canada's Wonderland* and one of the original 4 roller coasters that were at the Park when it opened in 1981. It is the longest single track wooden coaster in Canada at 3559 feet (1,085M). A modified traditional "Out & Back" wooden coaster which features an upward spiraling helix, the ride was built by Curtis T. Summers and was modeled after a ride at Coney Island.

https://www.canadaswonderland.com/rides/Thrill-Rides/Mighty-Canadian-Minebuster

CHAPTER 4: MATURITY

Best

The word literally means "ripe, fully developed, or having reached maximum potential."

THE THIRTEENITIES

http://www.dictionary.com/browse/maturity

ABCD

John Maxwell says, *"The greatest day in your life and mine is when we take total responsibility for our attitudes. That's the day we truly grow up."*

http://www.brainyquote.com/quotes/quotes/j/johncmaxw125843.html

CHAPTER 5: RESPONSIBILITY

Me

"If you are travelling with small children, put your oxygen mask on first before you assist them with theirs."

https://airodyssey.net/reference/inflight/

This life principle is uniquely illustrated in the May 8, 2005, story of *The Statue of Responsibility* by Caleb Warnock published in the *Daily Herald* of Provo, Utah. Warnock writes:

http://www.heraldextra.com/news/statue-of-responsibility/article_21e93a1f-94db-5533-9e5c-0560fff08972.html

"Most people do not really want freedom, because freedom involves responsibility, and most people are frightened of responsibility."

http://shimercollege.wikia.com/wiki/Fake_Quotes_Project/Freud/Most_people_do_not_really_want_freedom

Energy

Author Stephen R. Covey said, *"While we are free to choose our actions, we are not free to choose the consequences of our actions."*

166

http://www.goodreads.com/quotes/763419-while-we-are-free-to-choose-our-actions-we-are

Josiah Stamp put it this way, *"It is easy to dodge our responsibilities, but we cannot dodge the consequences of dodging our responsibilities."*

http://www.brainyquote.com/quotes/quotes/j/josiahstam172554.html

CHAPTER 6: COMMUNITY

Tribe

We have all heard the African proverb that it takes a village to raise a child.

http://www.npr.org/sections/goatsandsoda/2016/07/30/487925796/it-takes-a-village-to-determine-the-origins-of-an-african-proverb

Involved

As a motorcyclist, I have attended several of the famous Friday the 13th bike events in Port Dover, Ontario.

http://www.pd13.com/pages/1354815191/Origins

Support

Author M. Scott Peck wrote, *"There can be no vulnerability without risk; there can be no community without vulnerability; there can be no peace, and ultimately no life, without community."*

http://www.habitsforwellbeing.com/20-inspirational-quotes-on-vulnerability/

THE THIRTEENITIES

CHAPTER 7: GENEROSITY

Give

When I was a youth worker, I would organize service projects with different charitable agencies. One such agency was Ray of Hope in Waterloo Region, Ontario.

http://www.rayofhope.net/content/community-centre

The Hard Rock Café's motto is "Love all. Serve all."

https://www.hardrockhotels.com/culture.htm

CHAPTER 8: HUMILITY

Assist

One of his records that remains (at the time of the writing of this book) is being the all-time assist leader. In 1,487 games he scored 894 goals, but he assisted on 1,963 goals—an unbelievable 1.32 assists-per-game average over the span of his career.

https://www.nhl.com/news/the-great-ones-23-unbreakable-records/c-585698

Vertigo

BPV is caused when there is a disruption in the semicircular canals or the tubes in your inner ear.

http://www.healthline.com/health/benign-positional-vertigo

In his book *The Little Minister*, James Matthew Barrie reminds us all that, *"Life is a long lesson in humility."*

http://www.litquotes.com/quote_author_resp.php?AName=James%20M.%20Barrie

168

CHAPTER 9: INTEGRITY

Trivia

Another "wheel" illustration I often use in my keynote speaking is the wheel pattern on a Trivial Pursuit game board. The game was created by two Canadian men, Chris Haney and Scott Abbott, and was released in 1982.

http://www.ideafinder.com/history/inventions/
trivialpursuit.htm

CHAPTER 10: PURITY

Water

I had the chance to attend a Children's Groundwater Festival with my son on a school trip when he was in grade five (in the middle of his tweendom).

http://www.wwcgf.com/

Truth

A colleague and friend of mine named Tim used a phrase in a training seminar that I will always remember: "The truth will often hurt, but it never harms."

Tim Bailey and I have been friends, golf buddies, and communicators for many years. We have shared the stage presenting seminars to parents and youth workers numerous times.

CHAPTER 11: TENACITY

Hockey

When I think back on my childhood, I remember my hockey coach's words of wisdom. After a loss, he said something like this:

"Boys, in this game you will lose as many times as you will win. Either way, when you leave this room and the door hits your butt on the way out, the game is over. The key is to learn not only how to celebrate the victories, but to learn from the losses and be better prepared to play the next game. In hockey, it is not how big you are. It is not how strong you are. It is not even how skilled you are, or how well you are coached. It is always about how tough you are. It is about how big your heart is. It is about respecting yourself, your teammates and coaches, the referees, and even your opponents. In hockey, it is often the team with the most tenacity who wins. So we all walk out of this room with our heads up."

This speech is a compilation of thoughts I remember my coaches saying to me over the years. I have been blessed to have had a number of great coaches growing up in Kitchener Minor Hockey http://kitchenerminorhockey.com/

Bus

The actions of Mrs. Rosa Parks remind me of the value of tenacity.

http://www.biography.com/people/rosa-parks-9433715

Fail

I was fascinated to read an article about hockey goalie coach David Marcoux and the five Rs he teaches goalies to do after being scored on: release, relax, review, regroup, and refocus.

http://www.sourceforsports.com/Article/2370/A-Goalies-5Rs.aspx

CHAPTER 12: FLEXIBILITY

Dreams

Statically, the chances are very low.

Here are a few articles that address statistical chances of making the NHL

http://www.huffingtonpost.com/emily-cornelius/how-hard-is-it-to-make-it_b_5803634.html

http://www.totalsportsmgmt.com/pro-hockey/

106

Several years ago, I conducted a funeral service for a man named Gordon who was born in October 1905 and died in May of 2012.

Gordon's family has graciously allowed me to share his story.

CHAPTER 13: AUTHENTICITY

Swords

The Lord of the Rings, J. R. R. Tolkien

http://tolkiengateway.net/wiki/The_Lord_of_the_Rings

Chris Hogan once said, *"Somebody somewhere is in need of you becoming what you were destined to be. The only question is if you will do your part."*

THE THIRTEENITIES

From a tweet from, @ChrisHogan360 August 1, 2012

Challenge

In the book, *The Essential Bennis*, author Warren Bennis writes:

"To be authentic is literally to be your own author (the words derive from the same Greek root), to discover your native energies and desires, and then find your own way of acting on them. When you have done that, you are not existing simply to live up to an image posited by the culture or by family tradition or some other authority. When you write your own life, you have played the game that was natural for you to play."

The Essential Bennis, by Warren G. Bennis with Patricia Ward Biederman: John Wiley & Sons, Aug 10, 2009. Page 213

As someone once said, *"Always be who you are, and say what you feel, because people who mind don't matter, and people who matter don't mind."*

http://quoteinvestigator.com/2012/12/04/those-who-mind/

CHAPTER 14: SPIRITUALITY

Quest

North Americans today is that they are "spiritual but not religious."

http://news.nationalpost.com/holy-post/organized-religion-on-the-decline-growing-number-of-canadians-spiritual-but-not-religious

http://www.pewforum.org/religious-landscape-study/religious-denomination/spiritual-but-not-religious/

172

Faith

James 2:26, it says, *"As the body without the spirit is dead, so faith without deeds is dead."*

The Holy Bible, New International Version. Grand Rapids: Zondervan House. 1984

Heaven

"Thy kingdom come, Thy will be done, on Earth as it is in heaven."

Matthew 6:10, *The Holy Bible*, New International Version. Grand Rapids: Zondervan House. 1984

CHAPTER 15: CURIOSITY

Story

I once heard someone say, *"If you stop learning today, you will stop growing tomorrow."*

I cannot confirm the source of this quote.

Albert Einstein once said, *"Do not grow old, no matter how long you live. Never cease to stand like curious children before the Great Mystery into which we were born."*

http://www.goodreads.com/quotes/244559-do-not-grow-old-no-matter-how-long-you-live

CHAPTER 16: CREATIVITY

Birth

"In the beginning, God created..."

THE THIRTEENITIES

Genesis 1:1, *The Holy Bible*, New International Version. Grand Rapids: Zondervan House. 1984

CHAPTER 17: THE COMING OF AGE CEREMONY.

The Rite of Confirmation practiced by Roman Catholic Church.

https://www.loyolapress.com/our-catholic-faith/ sacraments/confirmation/history-and-development-of-sacrament-of-confirmation

Or the Jewish Bar Mitzvah or Bat Mitzvah ceremonies.

http://www.jewfaq.org/barmitz.htm

CHAPTER 18: FINALLY

Love

The ethic of love is woven into all the religious traditions of the world:

http://www.dummies.com/religion/exploring-religious-ethics-in-daily-life/

Symphony

One little girl whom he had taught the clarinet was now the state governor. She walked to the podium and said:

> *"Rumor had it that Mr. Holland was always working on this symphony of his. And this was going to make him famous, rich, probably both. But Mr. Holland isn't rich, and he isn't famous at least not outside of our little town. So it might be easy for him to think himself a failure. And he would be wrong, because I think he's achieved a success far beyond riches and fame. Look around you. There is not a life in this room that you have not touched. And each*

one of us is a better person because of you. We are your symphony, Mr. Holland. We are the melodies and the notes of your opus. And we are the music of your life."

http://www.imdb.com/title/tt0113862/quotes

Made in the USA
Middletown, DE
06 March 2017